CALLING UPON THE LORD

CALLING UPON THE LORD

By

DR. HARRY E. STANLEY II

A division of Squire Publishers, Inc.
4500 College Blvd.
Leawood, KS 66211
1/888/888-7696

Copyright 2001
Printed in the United States

ISBN: 1-58597-115-4

Library of Congress Control Number: 2001096814

A division of Squire Publishers, Inc.
4500 College Blvd.
Leawood, KS 66211
1/888/888-7696

*Dedicated
to my precious wife, Gina,
my lifetime faithful prayer partner*

TABLE OF CONTENTS

Before You Read This Book iii

Chapter 1 3

Chapter 2 12

Chapter 3 21

Chapter 4 31

Chapter 5 37

Chapter 6 45

Chapter 7 53

Chapter 8 59

Chapter 9 65

Chapter 10 73

Chapter 11 89

Chapter 12 95

Chapter 13 99

Conclusion 107

Appendix A 109

Appendix B 112

Bibliography 115

About the Author 116

Before you read this book,

"Are you 100% sure if you died today that you would go to Heaven?"

If you are 100% for sure that you are going to heaven, GREAT! If not let me tell you how you can be.

The Bible clearly states that all men will die and face judgment one day. *Hebrews 9:27 states, "It is appointed unto men once to die, but after this the judgment."* This includes you. This judgment that is mentioned concerns what we have done with Jesus Christ while physically alive on this planet. If you will, from your heart, acknowledge and turn from your sin, placing your faith in God's only begotten son, God the Son, Jesus Christ as your personal Savior you can be saved from your sins for all eternity.

I mentioned earlier that all will face the judgment. In order to be ready to face this judgment a person must believe and act upon the following truth from Scripture.

1. Turn from your sin.
   a. Admit you are a sinner.
   The Bible says in Romans 3:10, *"There is none righteous, no, not one."* Again in Romans 3:23, *"For all have sinned, and come short of the glory of God."* Have you ever humbly admit-

ted your faults to someone? The most important person in the universe to humble yourself before for your sin (All the bad things you have done—lying, stealing, cheating, immorality, murder, cursing, etc.) is God. God has already declared that you, along with every other human being born into this world, is a sinner with a heart that has a bent toward sinning. You must simply humble yourself before Him and agree with Him that He is righteous, holy, and perfect and you are a sinner. *"Behold, the LORD's hand is not shortened, that it cannot save; neither His ear heavy, that it cannot hear: but your iniquities have separated between you and your God, and your sins have hid His face from you, that He will not hear."* (Isaiah 59:1-2)

b. *Acknowledge there is a penalty for your sin.*
The Bible states in Romans 6:23, *"For the wages (penalty, what we earn) of sin is death; but the gift of God is eternal life through Jesus Christ our Lord."* If you'll notice all of this verse is one complete sentence or thought. God is comparing what we earn (wages of sin) with what He freely offers (gift of God). Notice we have earned death (eternal, not physical, separation from God eternally in hell). The contrast is eternal death with eternal life. Because all men have sinned all deserve to die and spend eternity in hell separated from God forever. Yet God offers to all men this gift of eternal life which is received when a person turns from their sin to trust Christ as their Savior. John 3:16 states, *"For God so loved the world, that He gave His only begotten Son, that whosoever believeth in Him should not perish but have everlasting life."* If you have never accepted Jesus Christ, God's Son, as your only way to heaven and you decided to stop reading this now, and you died today, you would drop into an everlasting place of torment called hell. "Why?" you ask. *"He that believeth on Him is not condemned: but he that believeth not is condemned already, because he hath not believed in the name of the only begotten Son of God."* (John 3:18) Spiritually, right now, you are condemned to an eternity

without God in everlasting punishment because you are a sinner. However, you do not have to go on another moment in this predicament.

2. Trust Jesus Christ as your Savior.
a. Acknowledge the payment of the penalty for your sin by Jesus Christ.

How did Jesus Christ, God's only begotten Son, pay the penalty for your sins already? *"But God commendeth (showed) His love toward us, in that, while we were yet sinners, Christ died for us."* (Romans 5:8) About 2,000 years ago Jesus Christ, God's Son, was supernaturally born of a virgin. He lived a perfect life. He never sinned, not once. He lived a righteous, holy life. The Jewish religious leaders of his day talked about living a righteous life and hated Him because they had an outward, partial conformity to God's Law and He perfectly kept God's Law. With a jealous hatred toward Jesus Christ, they had Him crucified. Not realizing that they were fulfilling the prophetic Scripture about their Jewish messiah which states, *"He [God] shall see of the travail of His [Jesus Christ] soul, and shall be satisfied: by His knowledge shall my righteous servant justify many; for He [Jesus Christ] shall bear their iniquities."* (Isaiah 53:11)

So why did Jesus Christ have to die? He had to shed His holy, spotless blood as the payment for the sins of all mankind to redeem (buy back) us (who are sold under sin and condemned to hell) back to Himself. *"Neither by the blood of goats and calves, but by His own blood He . . . obtained eternal redemption for us."* (Hebrews 9:12) Christ gave His physical life to pay for our eternal life. However, He rose again three days later from the grave conquering sin, death, and hell once and for all. Sometime after His resurrection, while speaking to the Apostle John, Jesus Christ confirmed this when He said, *"I am he that liveth, and was dead; and, behold, I am alive for evermore, Amen; and have the keys [power, authority over] of hell and death."* (Revelation 1:18) *b. Accept Jesus Christ as your personal Savior.*

If you personally accept and simply believe the above truth stated thus far, then in order for you to be 100% sure that you will go to heaven when you die, you must personally accept Christ as your Savior. *"That if thou shalt confess with thy mouth the Lord Jesus, and shalt believe in thine heart that God hath raised him from the dead, thou shalt be saved. For with the heart man believeth unto righteousness; and with the mouth confession is made unto salvation."* (Romans 10:9, 10)

God, according to His grace, is offering you the free gift of eternal life through Jesus Christ right now. It is purely a gift and you can do nothing to earn it. *"For by grace are ye saved through faith; and that not of yourselves: it is the gift of God: not of works, lest any man should boast."* (Ephesians 2:8, 9) All you have to do is simply reach out and take it, receive the gift! *"For whosoever shall call upon the name of the Lord shall be saved."* (Romans 10:13)

You can receive God's free gift of eternal life and be assured of a home in heaven forever, if, from your heart, you (while acknowledging the above truths) would pray a simple prayer to God simply like the following prayer:

"Dear Lord Jesus, I know that I am a sinner and I deserve to die and go to hell for all eternity to pay for my sins. Thank you for dying on the cross willingly to pay the penalty for my sins. I, here and now, on _____(date) accept your free gift of forgiveness of those sins. I ask you now to come into my heart and save me and give me eternal life. Amen."

If you just prayed the above prayer, you need to tell someone today. *"For the scripture saith, Whosoever believeth on him shall not be ashamed."* (Romans 10:11) Please take a moment and write me and let me know what you have done as a result of reading this today so that I can rejoice with you, pray for you, and send you some literature that will help you get grounded in your new faith in Christ. When I was 13 years old, I personally knelt by my bed at home and prayed a prayer similar to this one Sunday evening after church. The next day I told my parents about my decision to receive Christ and the following Sunday I went before my church and made my private decision public by telling others. May I encourage you to do this as well.

Although the enemy (the devil) will try to convince you later that this was not important or "You never really received Jesus Christ as your Savior," remember what God's Word says, *"And this is the record, that God hath given to us eternal life, and this life is in his Son. He that hath the Son hath life; and he that hath not the Son of God hath not life. These things have I written unto you that believe on the name of the Son of God, that ye may know that ye have eternal life."* (1 John 5:11-13)

Your decision to accept Christ as your personal Savior is the most important decision you will ever make in your life. Accepting Jesus Christ as your Savior is only a one time decision. Once you are confident you have accepted Christ as your Savior, you should start attending a local, Bible-believing church. You should start reading/studying your Bible daily (please contact me if you need one). You should start praying and talking with the Lord daily. These events, when they become a habit for you, will help you to grow spiritually and closer to God in your daily walk with Him. May God continue to bless you.

Dr. Harry E. Stanley II

What does it mean to "Call upon the name of the LORD"?

"For whosoever shall call upon the name of the Lord shall be saved."

—Romans 10:13—

A FEW WEEKS AGO my wife and I went out soul-winning to a development of new homes. We knocked first at a large, two-story house on the corner (our only house that evening), and a 15-year-old young man named Seth answered the door. Seth was not in the habit of attending church and went to the local public high school. When he told us his name, I was quick to tell him that his name was found in the Bible. I asked him if he had ever seen it before and he said no but he had heard of it. I then showed him in the Bible (Genesis 4:25-16) where his name was found, *"And Adam knew his wife again; and she bare a son, and called his name Seth: For God, said she, hath appointed me another seed instead of Abel, whom Cain slew. And to Seth, to him also there was born a son; and he called his name Enos: then began men to call upon the name of the LORD."* Those verses in Genesis were how I began sharing the gospel.

I began by showing Seth his name, but easily moved to the gospel with the last phrase of verse 26, *"Then began men to call upon the name of the LORD."* I had not been expecting the introduction to go so smoothly but this verse tied a perfect knot around the simple gospel with the final verse of Scripture being Romans 10:13 which states, *"For whosoever shall call upon the name of the Lord shall be saved."* The phrase in Scripture that became the silver cord for the gospel presentation was simply, "call upon the name of the LORD." Both Seth, and a friend of his who showed up while we were witnessing, prayed to accept Christ as their Savior.

While I was sharing the gospel with those young men, God pressed upon my heart the impact of that phrase, "call upon the name of the LORD." Have you ever been impacted not simply by this phrase but by its action? Has there ever been a point in your life when you called on the name of the LORD to be saved? You might be asking yourself, "Saved? From what?" Let me ask these questions: "Have you ever acknowledged your sin and asked Jesus Christ to save you?" "Are you 100% sure if you died today that you would go to heaven?" If not, please read the front section of this book where I simply explain the same truth from the Scriptures that I shared with Seth and his friend the night they trusted Jesus Christ as their personal Savior.

Before we left Seth's home, my wife and I gave both of those young men Bibles and explained to them that they needed to make their decisions public. We invited them to church and shared with them how to have their own personal devotions so that daily they could continue to call upon the name of the LORD. Since then, I have felt directed to personally study the Scriptures more in depth as to what it means to *call on the name of the Lord*. In essence it is addressing the Creator of this universe and then sharing with Him what our thoughts, needs, goals, burdens, ambitions, desires, requests and gratitude to Him might be at that exact moment in time. It has many implications and can be brought about by varying circumstances, yet all with the desired result of God hearing us and giving an answer. In the most basic term, "calling on the name of the Lord" is prayer.

Why don't we spend more time calling on the name of the Lord?

*"And there is none that calleth upon thy name,
that stirreth up himself to take hold of thee:
for thou hadst hid thy face from us,
and hast consumed us, because of our iniquities."*
Isaiah 64:7

HAVE YOU EVER found yourself not looking forward to spending time alone with your Heavenly Father and wondered why? The Scriptures give some direct comments concerning why men do not call upon the name of the Lord.

We are Heavy with Sleep

One reason that men do not call upon God is because spiritually they are counting sheep or heavy with sleep. God's choice of words in Isaiah 64:7 is interesting, *"And there is none that calleth upon thy name, that stirreth up himself to take hold of thee."* The word "stirreth" here deals specifically with a person who has been asleep. They are stirred up or awakened. It literally means the opening of the eyes, to wake or to waken.

Sin has a way of putting a man to sleep spiritually just as a mother does her baby when she rocks him to sleep at night. What is it about rocking a baby to sleep that has this effect?

The baby is gently caressed and held close so that it is distracted and relaxed enough to feel secure in its surroundings. The further a man goes in his sins, the more the surroundings become familiar and the more he needs to be spiritually stirred or awakened.

Any believer can find himself in this state if he is not careful. One of the Old Testament prophets turned his back on God and rejected God's direction for his life; in fact, he ran from God. His name was Jonah. Jonah, having been commanded by God to go to the wicked city of Ninevah and preach truth and judgment from God on their great sins, chose to disobey God and go in the opposite direction.

While disobeying God, Jonah boarded the ship headed for Tarshish (which was the opposite direction of where God had sent him); the gentle rocking motion of the ship made it all too easy for Jonah to check out and go find a comfortable place to sleep. The Bible says in the latter part of Jonah 1:5, *"But Jonah was gone down into the side of the ship; and he lay, and was fast asleep."*

But God was not finished with Jonah, so he sent a heathen messenger to awaken his chosen messenger. Jonah 1:6 says, *"So the shipmaster came to him, and said unto him, 'What meanest thou, O sleeper? Arise, call upon thy God, if so be that God will think upon us, that we perish not'."* Notice here that Jonah is addressed as, "O sleeper." The word sleeper has a root meaning of: to stupefy, to be fast asleep, or to be in a deep sleep. Jonah was out like a light and sleeping like a log. But God wanted to use Jonah in a great way and would not leave him alone. God had a mission for Jonah and He had chosen Jonah to do His work. Jonah was fast asleep and needed someone to remind him to "call upon the Lord." So God used this heathen shipmaster, whose vessel was in the midst of a storm, to redirect Jonah's attention back to his God.

Christian, do you find yourself in the same position as the prophet Jonah? Have you turned aside from some direction of

God in your life? Has your sin rocked you and cuddled you to spiritual lethargy? Is your life filled with storms that have spiritually shaken those around you? You need to heed the message of the shipmaster to probe your heart, "What meanest thou, O sleeper? Arise, call upon thy God." The word "arise" here has the connotation of, "to rise, to lift up, to raise up, to stand up, or to stir up." The message of our Shipmaster is for us to awake, to get up, to be spiritually stirred up from the lethargy calming and cradling us in our sinful circumstances that have dimmed our view of God and hindered our sensitivity to His voice. It is time for you to call upon your God!

We are Hardened with Sin

The Bible tells us the second reason that men do not call on the name of the Lord is the sins they commit. Just as Adam and Eve hid from God in the Garden of Eden when the Lord sought them, some shy away from speaking to the Lord because of sin in their lives. Psalm 53:4 states, *"Have the workers of iniquity no knowledge? who eat up my people as they eat bread: they have not called upon God."* The description here is twofold: (1) Workers of iniquity, and (2) who eat up my people as they eat bread. It is also to be noted that they have not called upon God.

Look now at why they do not call on God. Specifically, they are workers of iniquity. The word *workers* has the connotative meaning of: to do something systematically or habitually and especially to practice. The word "iniquity" simply means sin (or a willful transgression of the law of God) and carries with it the idea of wickedness, evil, vanity, injustice or mischief. The workers of iniquity, as described here in Psalm 53:4, are persons who habitually practice sin.

Notice, too, that the sin is not specified as being public or private; it is simply stated as being sin. Lost people do not seem to have much preference as to whether or not they practice sin in public or in private unless it is reprehensible and unacceptable to society, such as murder or adultery. Homosexuals used to keep their sins private, and some still do; however, many in the world flaunt it in public. Christians, on the other hand, tend to be conscientiously concerned with their public testimony, and rightly should be. However, many times they are not as careful in private; for instance, what they view on television or listen to on the radio. It is possible that this could be true of you, the reader, in your own personal life. If so, you are not calling on God because of your iniquity.

Also, today some families are in the habit of verbally abusing one another with hurtful words or emotionally withholding love from one another, choosing to return evil for evil. This often happens in the privacy of a home towards a spouse or a child, yet would never be tolerated outside the home in society or in the workplace. Men, especially, need to be careful to avoid such behavior toward their wives and children because it is in direct opposition to Scripture. I Peter 3:7 says, *"Likewise, ye husbands, dwell with them according to knowledge, giving honor unto the wife, as unto the weaker vessel, and as being heirs together of the grace of life; that your prayers be not hindered."*

I once had the opportunity to lead a man to Christ whose wife was about to take the children and leave the home because he was verbally and emotionally abusive. In fact, that very night, before he got saved, the lady had already determined the next day she was going to leave if something drastically good did not happen. It did! Her husband got saved! For the next month, every time I saw the man, his wife, or his children, they all had beaming smiles on their faces. The private sins in the home had ceased. The man, who had been a member of a church for 10 years, said, as he described his prayer life, "It was just like God in heaven had placed a wall up and every prayer I prayed was deflected right back at me." After his salvation he went home, humbled himself before his wife and children, and asked them to forgive him. They did, and it was so exciting to see what God was doing in that home. When he stopped being a worker of iniquity (of course, a change occurred at salvation), he began to pray more, and as I discipled him over the next few months, he gave testimony to many prayers being answered.

We are responsible to God, as his children, for what we do. God wants us to make a whole-hearted effort to live godly, holy and separated lives. Answered prayer is a benefit of such living. Yet we fail to pray because of the sin we commit. Isaiah 64:7 confirms in stating, *"And there is none that calleth upon thy name, that stirreth up himself to take hold of thee: for thou hadst hid thy face from us, and hast consumed us, because of our iniquities."* Why do people not call upon God? The answer is simple — because of the sins they commit.

Although people have different reasons they do not call upon God, these reasons do not negate the fact that they should be calling upon Him. When we call upon God there are certain benefits that we acquire. He will respond to us.

He will Hear us Sovereignly

Something will happen when we call upon God. As we draw near to God and call upon the name of the Lord, we see two responses of God in Scripture. First, we see that God will hear us. Jeremiah 29:12 records God saying, *"Then shall ye call upon me, and ye shall go and pray unto me, and I will hearken unto you."* God says it right here. It is a promise in Scripture just for you. In context, it applies directly to the nation of Israel who had turned their back on God, stopped listening to Him and become sin-ridden and enslaved to their enemies at Babylon. Just as God said that He would hear them, He wants you to know that He will hear you, too. If it has been a while since you have called upon God, turn back and do it now. God's message to you is that if you call upon Him, He will hearken to you; He will hear you.

He will Heal us Supremely

Not only will He hear you but *our* God also will heal you. The Bible says in Psalm 86:5, *"For thou, Lord, art good, and ready to forgive; and plenteous in mercy unto all them that call upon thee."* We will find what we need when we call upon the Lord. In Hebrews 4:16 the writer says, *"Let us therefore come boldly unto the throne of grace, that we may obtain mercy, and find grace to help in time of need."* When we see these two verses together, we cannot help but realize that when we call upon the Lord we will obtain His mercy tailor-made to our needs.

Walter Knight tells the following story about mercy. Shortly after Queen Victoria succeeded to the throne of England, the Lord Chamberlain presented her several documents that required her signature. Among them was a paper pertaining to a man who had committed a crime, and who had been sentenced to death. The queen's signature was needed for his execution to be carried out. "And must I become a party to his death?" Chamberlain responded, "I fear it is so unless Your Majesty desires to exercise her royal prerogative of mercy?" To her delight, she was informed that she had the power to pardon the condemned man. "As an expression of the spirit in which I desire to rule, I will exercise my royal prerogative," she said. She wrote the word "Pardoned" on the document and the prisoner was set free.[1]

Just as Queen Victoria could pardon a man who had been sentenced to death, so God wants us to know that as His dear children (as His servants, as His saints) we can come to Him and know that He will give us the mercy that we need no matter how great that need may be. Psalm 86:5 says that the Lord is plenteous in mercy unto all them who call upon Him. This word "plenteous" describes God's mercy to us as "abundant, exceedingly full, great, multiplied, and sufficient." No matter what our need is, when we call upon God, His mercy will be plenteous and sufficient to meet it.

When we call upon the Lord, He will heal us because He is

good and ready to forgive. He is waiting for us to come back to Him and to call upon Him when we have strayed. He is ready and waiting for us to call upon Him when we have sinned because He is a kind and loving God. He is ready to forgive us of our sin. He is ready to pardon us or to spare us of the furthered consequences of our sin if we will call upon Him.

So how about it my friend, will you call upon Him today? How long has it been since you have called upon Him? When is the next time that you will call upon Him? Please make it soon.

Commitment Prayer

Heavenly Father, thank you so much for your promises in Scripture for those who call upon your name. Please forgive me for allowing my sin to distance me from you and hinder me from calling on your name. Please forgive me for allowing myself to be gently distracted by the rocking motion of my circumstances. Help me be stirred to call upon you right now. Thank you for your promise that you will hear and that you will heal those who call upon your name. Please forgive me and grant to me the plenteous mercy you have for me right now. In Jesus' name I pray, Amen.

---

[1] Tan, Paul Lee. *Encyclopedia of 15,000 Illustrations.* Dallas, TX: Bible Communications, 1683.

Why Do We Call Upon God?

"Then shall ye call upon me and ye shall go and pray unto me, and I will hearken unto you."
Jeremiah 29:12

"Evening, and morning, and at noon, will I pray, and cry aloud: and he shall hear my voice."
Psalm 55:17

MANY TIMES as we read through the Psalms we find the *Psalmist* describing his prayer life, as is the case *here* in our text. David listed three separate times in his day that he worshipped God in prayer. Along with the recounting of these prayer times he also reveals why he prays: "And he shall hear my voice." This is a wonderful example of a believer who exercised his faith in God by communicating with Him. One might define prayer as "close, intimate fellowship (communion) between God and self, or a one-on-one dialogue with the Creator." When we get together with fellow believers at church, we most appreciate the time we have to speak to one another. We share the events of each other's week and relate what God has taught us or how He has blessed us. Oftentimes, during the week, we call to check on one another's health or well-being. We even make long distance calls to relatives or close friends to find out how they are doing and what is happening in their lives. This is fellowship. In *each* of these instances, *each* person takes time to talk and time to listen. Why do we speak to one another? We do so because we know that the other will listen. None of these conversations are one-sided. They are all two-way. Likewise, the time that we spend with God in prayer should not be one-sided either. It should be a time when we separate ourselves from all that is occurring and take time to be with God.

Prayer is meant to be a time of fellowship with our Creator just as it was for Adam and Eve in the Garden of Eden. We learn from Genesis 3:8 that God did not simply create mankind and then leave him to himself; He spent time communing with him. The passage states, *"And they heard the voice of the Lord God walking in the garden in the cool of the day: and Adam and his wife hid themselves from the presence of the Lord God amongst the trees of the garden."* Of course, Adam and Eve hid themselves because they knew they were guilty of disobeying God's command not to eat of the tree of the knowledge of good and evil. When they disobeyed God's spoken Word, they died spiritually. This made them to be sinful by nature and broke their fellowship with God. It also affected the nature of *all other* humans who would be born: they too became sinners. Romans 5:12 confirms this when it states, *"Wherefore, as by one man sin entered into the world, and death by sin; and so death passed upon all men, for that all have sinned."* Thus, while prayer is an exercise of faith in God and a time of fellowship with God, an overriding purpose of prayer is the need for man to experience the forgiveness of sin.

To Experience the Forgiveness of Sin

Amos 3:3 asks a question, *"Can two walk together, except they be agreed?"* In context, this was a question that God was directing toward the nation of Israel who had backslidden in its relationship with Him. He asks this questions just after making the statement in Amos 3:2, *"Therefore I will punish you for all your iniquities* [sins]." God cannot fellowship with sinful man because God is holy. Adam and Eve in the garden understood this having disobeyed God (and having a guilt-ridden conscience) they hid from God instead of walking and talking with Him. This is also confirmed elsewhere in Scripture concerning all humanity. Romans 3:10 states, *"As it is written, there is none righteous, no, not one"*; and Romans 3:23 reads, *"For all have sinned, and come short of the glory of God."* Man's sin has separated him from God. Every human being finds himself in this predicament. However, God's desire is that no one remain in this condition, but that each person turn from his sin to God for forgiveness of sin and eternal salvation. Romans 6:23 states it this way: *"For the wages of sin is death; but the gift of God is eternal life through Jesus Christ our Lord."* The apostle Peter, when addressing the religious leaders of Israel, said in Acts 5:31, *"Him [Christ] hath God exalted with his right hand to be a Prince and a Savior, for to give repentance to Israel, and forgiveness of sins."* This statement was made to a corporate nation needing to turn back to God from their sins but each of us must individually experience God's forgiveness of our sins. Ephesians 1:7 states, *"In whom we have redemption through his blood, the forgiveness of sins, according to the riches of his grace"*; and II Peter 3:9 concurs: *"The Lord is not slack concerning his promise, as some men count slackness; but is long-suffering to us-ward, not willing that any should perish, but that all should come to repentance."*

The joy of experiencing the forgiveness of sins is having a clear conscience. The writer of Hebrews said in Hebrews 9:14, *"How much more shall the blood of Christ, who through the eternal Spirit offered himself without spot to God, purge your conscience from dead works to serve the living God?"* When Adam and Eve sinned in the garden and hid themselves from God, it was because they had a guilty conscience. After they faced their sin and received their punishment, God covered their bodies with the skins of animals. Their guilty conscience was purged.

Reader, have you experienced the forgiveness of your sins? Have you ever personally admitted to the God of this universe that you are a sinful being and acknowledged in your heart that there is an eternal punishment for your sin? If you have not, I encourage you to stop now and do this.

Bud Robinson, a cowboy who became an old time preacher, recalls the time that he accepted Christ as his Savior in a camp meeting.

> Deep conviction had settled down on me the second day. I felt that I was lost. One day the preachers asked the workers to go down into the crowd and find a sinner and pray for him wherever they found him. A beautiful old mother with white hair and the finest face I ever saw came through the crowd. She looked like you could take a rag and wipe heaven off her face. She found me sitting on the back bench. There was no need of her saying, "Young man, are you a sinner?" She looked at me and knew no Christian ever looked like I did. She went down before me on her knees and put her hands upon my bare knees where they were sticking through my dirty overalls and prayed for me as loudly as she could. The devil got up and said, "If you don't give her a cussing she never will quit." But it seemed the Lord said, "Don't you cuss this woman; she is praying for your lost soul." Then it seemed to me the devil said, "If you don't get up and run they are going to get you." But, beloved, God had come on the scene. I tried to get up, but could not get off of the bench. It seemed as though I were glued to it while the devil hissed in my face. That beautiful mother prayed louder and louder, and finally began to shout; and rising on her knees she commenced to beat me on the head until I thought I was going to sink through the ground into the pit. The old mother shouted as long as she wanted

to, and when she finally arose she looked like she was half glorified."

The arrow of conviction stuck in Bud's heart. That night, in the midst of a tremendous altar service, such as were expected in the old-time camp meetings, he made his way to the place of prayer, taking with him such a burden for sins as one cannot long carry and live. There was around that altar such a prayer meeting that afterward Bud described it as "a life and death struggle." At the close of that prayer meeting Bud Robinson was converted and blessed with such an ecstasy that he could never describe it except by saying, "the bottom of heaven dropped out and my soul was filled with light and joy." [1]

To Enjoy Fellowship with God

Another purpose for prayer is to enjoy fellowship with God. The Psalmist wrote in Psalm 42:1, *"As the hart* [deer] *panteth after the water brooks, so panteth my soul after thee, O God."* People, not plants or animals, are designed to have fellowship with God. This is how God designed us. Often believers are reminded of the words to the hymn, *In the Garden,* which reads:

> I come to the garden alone, While the dew is still on the roses; And the voice I hear falling on my ear, the Son of God discloses. And He walks with me, and he talks with me, And He tells me I am His own; And the joy we share as we tarry there, None other has ever known.

We need to spend time alone in fellowship with God. Each individual needs to spend his personal time alone with God.

One person who stands out in the pages of *Scripture*, because he walked with God and enjoyed fellowship with God, was Enoch. Genesis 5:21-24 tell us: *"And Enoch lived sixty and five years, and begat Methuselah: And Enoch walked with God after he begat Methuselah three hundred years, and begat sons and daughters; And all the days of Enoch were three hundred sixty and five years; And Enoch walked with God: and he was not; for God took him."* Twice Enoch's personal relationship with God is mentioned specifically. In a great time of wickedness (not too many years before the flood that destroyed the previous population of this planet), Enoch, a holy, separated man of character, walked with God. Charles Spurgeon, describing this aspect of Enoch's life, wrote,

> He lived toward the close of those primitive times wherein long lives had produced great sinners, and great sinners had invented great provocations of God. Do not complain, therefore, of your times and of your neighbors and other surroundings, for amid them all you may still walk with God.[2]

Enoch walked with God and enjoyed fellowship with God. This fellowship with God was so complete that he took a stand for right against all the wrong of his day. Jude verses 14 and 15 quote Enoch as saying,

> *Behold, the Lord cometh with ten thousands of his saints, To execute judgment upon all, and to convince all that are ungodly among them of all their ungodly deeds which they have ungodly committed, and of all their hard speeches which ungodly sinners have spoken against him.*

Enoch walked with God and Enoch enjoyed fellowship with Him. Enoch had to have disdained the sin of his day as did the God with whom he fellowshipped. He is only one of two men mentioned in Scripture who did not taste death. *"He walked with God and he was not; for God took him."* Oh, to have a walk with God that would influence the world; that would cause others to miss you when you are gone. Do you enjoy fellowship with God, my fellow Christian? Do you take the time to pray as you ought? Prayer is fellowship with God.

To Exercise Faith in God

In Matthew 21:21-22, Jesus said,

Verily I say unto you, If ye have faith, and doubt not, ye shall not only do this which is done to the fig tree, but also if ye shall say unto this mountain, Be thou removed, and be thou cast into the sea; it shall be done. And all things, whatsoever ye shall ask in prayer, believing, ye shall receive.

He first says, "If ye have faith." God wants to know uppermost if we have faith. He then adds that if we have faith in God that faith will be revealed through prayer. When there is a mountainous problem that needs to be removed to the sea, Jesus said, *"If ye have faith and doubt not ... whatsoever ye shall ask in prayer, believing, ye shall receive."* How exciting to know that during times of increased testing, Jesus encourages us to exercise our faith in God through prayer.

I once read a statement written by Warren Wiersbe in one of his books, "A faith that cannot be tested cannot be trusted." A man may say, "I'm the fastest man in the world"; but no one will believe him until he exercises his body on the track, racing against other runners and the clock. Yet Maurice Greene from Kansas could actually say that in truth. Whether seen at the Olympics or the trial stages (testing), he proved to everyone that he was the world's fastest man in the 100-meter dash in 2000. He beat not only all competitors but held the world record as well. He had faith; he exercised his faith. Now, that was in the physical; and Jesus wants us to show Him that we have faith in the spiritual by exercising our faith in prayer.

One Old Testament example of this is Moses leading the children of Israel out of Egypt. As the people saw the supernatural hand of God — first with the waters of the Red Sea standing as walls and then with those same waters crashing in a flood to destroy Pharaoh's army — they seemed to be living by faith in Moses and Moses' God. However, Moses appears to be the one who was exercising faith in God. When they came to Marah they found the waters there to be bitter; the people were not happy with Moses and complained against him. Exodus 15:24-25 says,

> *"And the people murmured against Moses, saying, What shall we drink? And he cried unto the Lord; and the Lord shewed him a tree, which when he had cast into the water, the waters were made sweet."*

Here we see Moses trusting in God through prayer. God tested his faith and it was secure. When Moses found himself in need he could depend on God; he prayed to God on behalf of the people and God answered his prayer. When we pray, our answers may not come as quickly; yet we must continue to exercise our faith in God. The more we exercise our faith in God, the stronger we will become. I'm sure that Maurice Greene did not just walk out onto the track one day and break the world record for speed in the men's 100-meter dash. He probably practiced often and prepared himself through rigorous exercise and healthy eating. He protected and preserved his physical health because he knew it was important to the accomplishment of his goal to be the fastest man in the world. If you are having trouble with little faith, it is probably because you have little exercise. Romans 10:17 states, *"So then faith cometh by hearing, and hearing by the Word of God."* Believing and acting upon this verse can encourage you to grow as a believer.

Three basic purposes of prayer are for us to experience the forgiveness of sin, to enjoy fellowship with God, and to exercise our faith in God. Reader, I ask you today, in which one of these areas does your prayer life need a jump-start? I trust you have experienced the forgiveness of your sins. If not, you can right now. Simply refer back to the beginning of this book. There contained is the scriptural truth necessary for your eternal salvation.

If you have already trusted Christ, then I ask you, are you enjoying daily fellowship with God in prayer? Are you walking with God as Enoch did? Is your faith being tested? Are you exercising your faith in God as you should?

Prayer Commitment

To trust Christ as your Savior and experience the forgiveness of sins, refer to the section at the beginning of this book entitled, "Are you 100% sure you are going to heaven?"

For believers:

Heavenly Father, thank you so much that you desire to have fellowship with me as your child. Help me to anticipate our daily time together in prayer and help me to trust you and to exercise my faith in you through prayer on a regular daily basis. In Jesus' name, amen.

---

[1] Chapman, J. B. *Bud Robinson, A Brother Beloved* (St. John, IN: Beacon Hill Press, 1989), 30-31.

[2] Spurgeon, Charles, *Men and Women of the Old Testament* (Chattanooga, TN: AMG Publisher, 1995), p. 22.

3

The Power of Prayer

"The effectual fervent prayer of a righteous man availeth much."
—James 5:16b—

HAVE YOU EVER WONDERED why sometimes your prayers do not seem to be answered by God while other times they do? Have you ever found yourself going to one specific friend or family member just because you know that when they pray their prayers seem to get answered more *readily* than yours or even others? Maybe you have determined that your mother or grandmother fits into the category of "prayer warrior." Have you ever asked yourself, "Why doesn't God answer my prayers as *readily* as He does their prayers?"

My grandmother, who is in her nineties, received Christ as her personal Savior in her early twenties not long after she was married. She followed my grandfather as God led him to pastor a church, travel as an evangelist, and go to Haiti as a missionary. God called my grandfather home after being a missionary for about fifteen years. That occurred over 35 years ago. My grandmother has since continued to walk with God; and when she grew older, she came to live with our family. As a little boy I can remember night after night when she would read me a Bible story and then pray with me before going to bed. It *sometimes* seemed that the prayer time was just as long, if not longer, than the story time. Yet our family knew that God would hear Grandmother when she prayed. We used to say, "She could get hold of Heaven!" It is the same today. Whenever I have a need for prayer in some area of my life, my grandmother is one of the first people I call and ask to pray for me. Often times, she will call and ask me what or how I am doing. Then she'll say, "I knew there was a reason God burdened my heart to pray for you."

Just as my grandmother has gained the reputation of being a "prayer warrior," so have many others, including prominent Old Testament figures. James, inspired by the Holy Spirit, illustrates the power of prayer through one of the many adventures in the life of the Old Testament prophet Elijah. James 5:17-18 states, *"Elias was a man subject to like passions as we are, and he prayed earnestly that it might not rain: and it rained not on the earth by the space of three years and six months. And he prayed again, and the heaven gave rain, and the earth brought forth her fruit."* Have you ever stopped to consider what the possibilities might be for it not to rain in the land of Israel for three years and six months? It must have been a supernatural event interwoven with the sureness of Elijah, the sin of King Ahab, and the sovereignty of Jehovah God. Elijah announced the event beforehand; Ahab was angered by it; and God acknowledged Elijah's word with no rain falling upon the land for three years and six months!

Different men through the ages have been known to be great men of prayer, men such as "Praying Hyde," George Mueller, and another more quiet man of prayer, the backbone of Charles Finney's revivals, Father Nash. How did these "prayer warriors" get their prayers answered in such a pronounced way? They tapped into the power of prayer. They became energized intercessors. What would it take for your prayer life to become this effective? You need to determine why you pray and whether or not your prayers are biblical.

An Energized Intercessor

This principle can be drawn from the two words in our English Bible "effectual fervent." These two words are actually translated from the Greek root word "energeo" which is the same word from which the English word "energy" is derived. This word has the denotative meaning of being active, efficient, effectual, to be mighty in, or simply to work. It demonstrates for us that there are prayers that can be prayed that are active. Often when a person finds themselves in a predicament to which they determine there is no human solution, they say, "All I can do now is pray." As if to say that prayer is not actively working to fulfill the desired goal or to obtain the object sought, this thinking is absolutely contrary to this meaning. In reality, "energeo" indicates a person is genuinely relying upon and yielding to the most influential force in the universe, God. Contextually, the energy here described is the energy that is actively and efficiently revealing God's mighty hand accomplishing His work. Think about the story recounted in James. How did Elijah know that it would not rain for three years and six months? How could he proclaim this unashamedly, yet respectfully, to the face of one of Israel's most wicked kings? His prayer was energized; it was not a "last resort," but rather a first resort. God chose to use Elijah as the mouthpiece proclaiming God's judgment upon his people. Elijah chose to yield in submission to God and prayed, in direct, divinely ordered power, for God's will for a nation: no rain for three years and six months. Then, he prayed again and it rained. James reminds us that it was this simple, yet *this* powerful.

Are your prayers as effective as Elijah's? They can be. God desires all of His children to be mighty in their prayer life, not just a select few. So why then do not all of us pray this effectively all of the time? Our prayers can be energized by different sources.

Selfish source for Prayer

One motivation for praying is self. Self-centeredness, selfishness, self-will, self goals, self dreams, self-made people, all of these word pictures describe the flesh. Earlier James described these types of prayers in James 4:3 when he wrote, *"Ye ask, and receive not, because ye ask amiss, that ye may consume it upon your own lusts."* Truthfully, what percentage of the prayers that you have prayed in the last week have been God-centered or Holy Spirit originated versus the percentage of prayers that have been self-centered or flesh/lust originated? This might also be reflected if we asked what percentage of our prayers were answered.

If you have become frustrated because it seems that God does not hear your prayers or answer them, then ask yourself, "Am I praying in accordance with God's will or trying to pray for God to work in accordance with my will?" Saul was on his way to Damascus to persecute the saints when Jesus Christ said to him in Acts 9:4-5, *"Saul, Saul, why persecutest thou Me? . . . it is hard for thee to kick against the pricks."* Without realizing it, fellow believer, when we are praying based on our own lusts or with selfish motives at the root of our prayers, we are not praying in accord once with God's will but rather against it. If you, as a parent, had a child that came to you with selfish requests over and over, would it be your greatest desire to grant their requests or to teach them how to be unselfish? So also is the case with our Heavenly Father. We must not continue asking amiss but must learn to pray effectually and fervently. So how do we do this?

Spirit-controlled prayer

The Holy Spirit must become the source of our prayers. The Bible teaches that the Holy Spirit should be the guide and energizer of our prayer requests in Romans 8:26-27 when it states, *"Likewise the Spirit also helpeth our infirmities: for we know not what we should pray for as we ought: but the Spirit itself maketh intercession for us with groanings which cannot be uttered. And he that searcheth the hearts [Christ] knoweth what is the mind of the Spirit, because he maketh intercession for the saints according to the will of God."* We know that something is the will of God, not simply through an overwhelming desire to pray for it, but when it, in accordance with Scripture, becomes the only desire. The Holy Spirit has only one mind on every matter of the believer's life. When we are praying in accordance with His will, instead of from selfish motives, it becomes a selfless matter. Instead of our needs and desires centering around our life, they begin to center around a much larger picture-God's divine plan and will.

The Holy Spirit helps our infirmities, or our weaknesses. In context, this word is pointing to our spiritual life, not our physical life. With this in mind, we realize that even in our greatest time of dependence upon God, we can be weak, praying only for that which seems best or right to us. However, God the Holy Spirit knows and understands the big picture and not just our situation; therefore, when we pray He comes to our aide during those times when He knows we are most in need, or failing to request that which is God's best for us (i.e., His perfect will).

A person who is praying a Spirit-led prayer is someone praying in tune with the Holy Spirit and not someone trying to pray God into tune with their desires. Are you willing to ask yourself right now, what is the one prayer request that is on your heart above any other? When you start praying to God and asking genuinely from your heart about that request, does your mind tend to think toward other ways that God could possibly answer it? If so, perhaps God is trying to show you His answer to the request that you are bringing before Him. Be sensitive and obedient to the still, small voice of God. Remember, if you are a born-again child of God you have the Holy Spirit living on the inside. He is the Spirit of Christ, the good Shepherd; He will not lead you astray because He knows what is the exact will of God for you in that situation. The litmus test for every prayer request is the Scripture. If God is redirecting a prayer request you bring to Him, then it can be confirmed in the Bible. Please do not become guilty of taking a verse out of context or misapplying it to your situation; but rather filter your request *through* the Word of God for confirmation, using two or three passages. After all, the Word of God is the only Spirit-breathed book we have. If we are praying a Spirit-led prayer, it will be confirmed through the Scriptures and we will have the peace that passes understanding as well as biblical understanding.

One such evangelist that was well known for praying Spirit-led prayers was Charles Finney. The following story is told in one biography of his life:

> While in prayer God revealed to Finney that he must go to the nearby town of Gouverneur. "Of the place, I knew nothing," said Mr. Finney, "except that there was much opposition to the revival in Antwerp. I can never tell how or why the Spirit of God made that revelation to me. But I knew then, and I have no doubt now, that it was a direct revelation from God to me . . . But in prayer the thing was all shown to me, as clear as light . . . that God would pour out His Spirit there."
>
> This is characteristic of Mr. Finney's contacts with spiritual illuminations. He learned to wait on God until the Divine plan unfolded to his thinking and then he acted speedily. Shortly, he saw a man from Gouverneur and told him of the revelation, asking him to pass word to the brethren that he would soon be over and to prepare "for the out-pouring of the Lord's Spirit." This seemed to be a step marked with unwarranted audacity, a faith step this man of God never failed to take when inwardly wrought upon by the Spirit. Religion there was of a low state and the messenger himself "as cold as an iceberg."
>
> In the Spirit's time, when the LaRaysville revival had

finished its soul-redeeming work, God said, "Go to Gouverneur; the time has come." First Finney sent his prayer-partner Father Nash ahead to prepare the people for his coming, and on the appointed time, after much prayer by the two workers, "there was a general turning out of the people."

When the majority of the Gouverneur people had been converted, Finney went to DeKalb, sixteen miles farther north, where the Methodists sometime before had a revival in which many people fell under divine power.[1]

God used Charles Finney to spark one of America's greatest revivals. What was the key? Spirit-led prayers. O, what God could do in our country today if more of its ministers got ahold of God praying Spirit-led prayers! Not only are Spirit-led prayers important but so are scripturally supported prayers.

Scripture-centered prayer

Can your request be seen in Scripture and supported as truth? Let us look at the biblical illustration in the context of our key verse of Scripture. James 5:16-18 states, *"Confess your faults one to another, and pray one for another, that ye may be healed. The effectual fervent prayer of a righteous man availeth much. Elias was a man subject to like passions as we are, and he prayed earnestly that it might not rain: and it rained not on the earth by the space of three years and six months. And he prayed again, and the heaven gave rain, and the earth brought forth her fruit."* As we look at this story in Scripture there are various facets to be considered. First, why would a prophet in Israel pray that God would withhold rain from the land of his people? Rain, in its season, was a blessing from God. Why did this prophet pray for the nation not to receive the blessing? Did he not care for the nation of Israel? Was not the well-being of the nation's agricultural and economic growth important to him? Was he not concerned that if there had been a drought in the land there might also be starvation and deprivation of physical needs? Simply put, one might be so bold as to say, "Elijah didn't really care for his nation like he should have cared. Instead of praying for judgment and the withholding of a blessing, Elijah should have been praying for God's mercy and forgiveness upon his nation." One simple question should be posed here, "Does this thinking align itself properly with Scripture?" And the answer would be: In other circumstances, possibly, but in this case the answer is no. Elijah was not only the most verbal spokesman for God in his day, but he was also the prophet hand-picked by God to be the spiritual leader for Israel. The king, King Ahab, was a wicked king and had led the nation down the sin-cursed path of practicing idolatry. The Bible clearly reveals this in 1 Kings 16:33, which reads, *"And Ahab made a grove; and Ahab did more to provoke the LORD God of Israel than all the kings of Israel that were before him."* It is just two verses after this statement in Scripture that Elijah can be seen confronting Ahab about this sin and sharing with him the resulting judgment that Elijah had prayed for Israel. Why did Elijah pray for judgment upon his nation? Was it simply an intense, emotional prayer because he was not in agreement with the political authority in power at the time or was it a Spirit-led prayer? Filtering this incident through the giving of the law to the nation of Israel, confirmation in Scripture can clearly be seen. In Leviticus 26:1-4 the Bible records, *"Ye shall make you no idols nor graven image, neither rear you up a standing image, neither shall ye set up any image of stone in your land, to bow down unto it: for I am the LORD your God. Ye shall keep my sabbaths, and reverence my sanctuary: I am the LORD. If ye walk in my statutes, and keep my commandments, and do them; Then I will give you rain in due season, and the land shall yield her increase, and the trees of the field shall yield their fruit."* According to this passage of Scripture, God commanded that Israel should not practice idolatry. A blessing for not practicing idolatry was rain in its due season. In light of our story, a person does not have to be a farmer to figure out that no rain for the space of three years and six months is not "rain in its due season." Again, as this story is *filtered through* the context of *Scripture,* we read in Deuteronomy 11:13-14, *"And it shall come to pass, if ye shall hearken diligently unto my commandments which I command you this day, to love the LORD your God, and to serve him with all your heart and with all your soul, That I will give you the rain of your land in his due season, the first and the latter rain, that thou mayest gather in thy corn, and thy wine, and thine oil."*

Twice now it becomes obvious that Elijah's prayer was Spirit-led. Israel was practicing idolatry in direct disobedience to the command and caution from God. Elijah simply confirmed in prayer what Israel had set in motion by their sinful practice. It is also just as obvious and important to note that what Elijah prayed came to pass. It was God's will that for the space of three and a half years Israel would receive no rain. Learning to pray Spirit-led prayers comes with practice. The more a person prays in accordance with God's will and submits to the direction of God's Holy Spirit, confirming his request scripturally, the more the person will see God answer his prayers. Not only was the first time that Elijah prayed important to God's will, but the second time he prayed (requesting for God to send the rain) was equally important. Israel turned back to God from serving Baal and slew 850 false prophets. At this time Elijah went to his knees, requesting rain from God in heaven; and it rained.

There was a lady attending our church who, on one occasion, became very ill and went to the doctor. He discerned the severity of her problem, but could not determine the cause. As the lady continued in her devotions before the Lord she came to the conclusion that hers was a situation that merited calling the elders to pray for her according to James 5:14, 15, and 16: *"Is any sick among you? let him call for the elders of the church; and let them pray over him, anointing him with oil in the name of the Lord: and the prayer of faith shall save the sick, and the Lord shall raise him up; and if he have committed sins, they shall be forgiven him. Confess your faults one to another, and pray one for another, that ye may be healed."* At the appointed time of the meeting, the lady shared that the Lord had kindly shown her that some personal habits had been the cause of her sickness, and that she had *confessed* this before Him. We prayed for her that she would be healed, and within a week it became evident that the Lord had healed her. I am not saying that God does not use the technological advancements in medicine He has allowed mankind to discover and practice; however, I am saying that God does answer prayer, especially prayer that is scripturally based. The most important aspect of our prayer life is that it be Spirit-controlled and Scripture-centered.

Questions to Ponder
1. Are the majority of my prayers being answered?
2. How often are my prayers self-centered?
3. How can I transition my prayer life to be Spirit-controlled praying?
4. Can I support my prayer request scripturally?

Commitment Prayer
Heavenly Father, I confess to you that many times I have come to you in prayer willfully, trying to change you. Will you please forgive me for being selfish and praying amiss? I yield my prayer life to you. I desire for the Holy Spirit to be in control of my prayer life and guide me in my requests. Please help me to request that which pleases You, is in accordance with Your will, and is supported by Your Word. In Jesus' name, amen.

---

[1] Miller, Basil. *Charles Finney* (Minneapolis, MN: Bethany House, 1991), 47-49.

4

We Must Learn to Pray Determined Prayers

"In the day of my trouble, I will call upon thee: for thou wilt answer me."

Psalm 86:7

D<small>R</small>. WILBUR CHAPMAN wrote to a friend: "I have learned some great lessons concerning prayer. At one of our missions in England the audience was exceedingly small; but I received a note saying that an American missionary was going to pray down God's blessing on our work. He was known as Praying Hyde. Almost instantly the tide turned. The hall became packed, and at my first invitation 50 men accepted Christ as their Savior. As we were leaving, I said, 'Mr. Hyde, I want you to pray for me.'

"He came to my room, turned the key in the door, and dropped on his knees, and waited five minutes without a single syllable coming from his lips. I could hear my own heart thumping, and his beating. I felt hot tears running down my face. I knew I was with God. Then, with upturned face, while the tears were streaming down, he said, 'O God.' Then for at least five minutes he was still again; and then, when he knew that he was talking with God, there came from the depths of his heart such petitions for me as I had never heard before. I arose from my knees knowing what real prayer was. We believe that prayer is mighty and we believe it as we never did before."[1]

Praying Hyde was the man whom we believers would deem in every sense of the word, "a prayer warrior." He spent his hours and days alone with God and God answered his prayers. What can we learn about John Hyde's prayer life just from his nickname? He was a determined man of prayer. His prayers were determined prayers that God heard and answered.

There are two aspects of a determined prayer life: time and trouble. Psalm 86:7 directs our attention to these aspects in stating, *"In the day of my trouble I will call upon thee: for thou wilt answer me."* This verse immediately points us to the heart of an individual, David, who had determined what he would do in the day of trouble. It goes without saying that David was a mighty warrior, whether in battle against another nation, such as the Philistines, or simply hand-to-hand combat with one such as Goliath. In fact, at the end of David's life, God said that he could not build the temple because of the blood on his hands. Yet we find these eternal words penned by the mighty warrior, King David: "In the day of trouble I will rally the troops." No. "In the day of trouble I will go to war." No. "In the day of trouble I will plan my strategy." No. *"In the day of trouble I will call upon thee for thou wilt answer me."* What made David a valiant warrior in battle was his determined prayers behind closed doors. David had determined that in the day, or the time, of his trouble he would call upon the name of the Lord. Are you determined in your prayer life like David was? What is it that you have determined you will do in the time of trouble? "I will call my stock broker." "I will call my boss." "I will call my mom." "I will call a friend." Or is the first person you would call upon, God? *"I will call upon Thee."*

Time

The writer of Ecclesiastes began a poem describing the different elements of an individual's life when he wrote the words of Ecclesiastes 3:1, *"To everything there is a season and a time to every purpose under the heaven."* Strangely enough, the writer of Ecclesiastes was Solomon, the son of King David. Solomon had learned some truths about the variety of events in a person's life as he grew up in King David's house. He could recall the time that his father left Jerusalem as his elder brother, Absalom, attempted to steal the throne. He could also remember when King David re-entered Jerusalem as the king and reacquired his throne. Most influential upon his life, however, was King David's response to these troubles. Solomon had to have noticed his father calling upon the name of the Lord on many occasions and allowing him to see the reality of Psalm 86:7 in his life: *"In the day of trouble I will call upon thee."* The first step necessary to having a *determined* prayer life is determining that there are certain times in our lives when we will call upon the name of the Lord.

Trouble

The next ingredient of a determined prayer is "trouble." This word is different than that word translated "distress" in Psalm 118:5 discussed in the previous chapter. This word *connotatively* means a narrowness or a tightness that becomes a rival or an adversary, adversity, affliction or anguish. This was the type of trouble that Joseph found himself in when his brothers hated him and continued to put him in tight places. First, they left him out and didn't accept him. Then, when he went looking for them, they put him in the pit. Finally, they sold him to the traveling band of Ishmaelites headed to Egypt. Many years later as they remembered the vividness of the way they wrongfully treated Joseph, their words to one another were (Genesis 42:21), *"We are verily guilty concerning our brother, in that we saw the anguish of his soul, when he besought us, and we would not hear, therefore is this distress come upon us."* They saw the "anguish" of his soul that they caused. This is the same word as "trouble" here in Psalm 86:7.

This word "trouble" is also the same word that David used to describe the many circumstances that King Saul had formulated against him while pursuing David and trying to take his life. David said in II Samuel 4:9-10, *"As the Lord liveth, who hath redeemed my soul out of all adversity, when one told me, saying, Behold, Saul is dead ...."* David could think back to the many different tight situations of trouble, adversity, and affliction afforded him as Saul sought his life. Saul tried to nail him to the wall with a javelin on two occasions. He sent men to surround the house and kill him in his bed at home. He chased him around a mountain. He followed him into the cave at Machpehlah. David's adversary made tough situations for him, yet David could say, *"As the Lord liveth, who hath redeemed my soul out of all adversity."* If it were not for these times of trouble in the life of David, we might not have many of the Psalms that were determined prayers of his when he called upon the name of the Lord.

J.G. Bowan tells the following story:

"One night during the Civil War in America, a stranger came to Henry Ward Beecher's house. It was night and Mrs. Beecher went to see who it was. She found a stranger muffled to the eyes, who asked to see the great preacher. He refused to give his name, and, because her husband's life was threatened at that time, Mrs. Beecher declined to receive him. She resumed upstairs and told her husband of the stranger at the door.

"Beecher never knew fear. He, at once, descended and admitted him. Later, when Mr. Beecher rejoined his wife, he told her that the muffled stranger was none other than Abraham Lincoln. He, too, was in a crisis. He needed prayer."[2]

The Civil War was a time of real adversity for the whole nation, especially for the President. He needed prayer; it is that simple. In our times of trouble, or adverse circumstances, we need to have already determined that we are going to pray; we are going to call on the name of the Lord.

The Psalmist had so determined to pray during the time of trouble because he was confident that God would answer his prayers. Do you have this same confidence and faith in God?

John Paton, missionary to the New Hebrides Islands-specifically to head hunting tribes, found himself in troubling, dangerous situations on many different occasions. Once he dared a local chief to place a curse on him to show the chief that John's God was more powerful. Nothing happened. On another occasion there had been a secret pact to kill John and some of his assistants, so they stayed inside their home on the missionary compound. However, on one occasion while tending his garden he faced a very tense circumstance. He recounted the following story:

Dangers again darkened around me. While working near my house, Miaki the war chief, his brother, and a large party of armed men surrounded me. They all had muskets beside their own native weapons. They watched me for some time in silence and then every man leveled a musket straight at my head. Escape was impossible. Speech would only have increased my danger. My eyesight came and went for a few moments. I prayed to my Lord Jesus to either protect me or take me home. I tried to keep working at my task, as no one was near me. In that moment as never before the words came to me, "Whatever you ask in My name, I will do it," and I knew that I was safe. Backing away a little from their position, no words spoken, they took up the same positions a little farther off, and they seemed to be urging one another to fire the first shot. Once again my dear Lord restrained them, and they withdrew.[3]

Our determined prayers are born out of two factors that weigh heavily upon our hearts, the time the trouble occurs in my life and the amount or type of difficulty that we experience. The Psalmist could state with all confidence, *"In the day of my trouble, I will call upon thee: for thou wilt answer me."*

At some point in our life God desires for us to obtain this same confidence and trust in Him.

Commitment Prayer

Heavenly Father, help my faith and confidence in you to be so strong that I will be determined to turn to you in prayer during my time of trouble. In Jesus' name, amen.

---

[1] Tan, Paul Lee. *Encyclopedia of 15,000 Illustrations.* Dallas, TX: Bible Communications, 2157.

[2] Ibid, 2168.

[3] Unseth, Benjamin. *John Paton* (Minneapolis, MN: Bethany House, 1996), 59-60.

5

We Must Call Upon the Lord in Times of Distress

"I called upon the Lord in distress:
the Lord answered me, and set me in a large place."
Psalm 118:5

ONE DAY a 20-year-old young man in a family from our church was at home talking to his father on the kitchen phone when he heard a loud "pop" from the basement. He went to the door leading downstairs, opened it, and found smoke coming up the stairwell. The fire in their basement had just opened to a large blaze when the fire neared a gas line that had a small hole in it. The fire in the basement began to rage and smoke began to billow throughout the house. The young man immediately called 911 and firefighters showed up shortly. Because of the son's rapid response they were able to extinguish the fire before major structural damage was done. No one else was in the house at the time so the fire resulted in no personal injuries. However, due to the intensity of the blaze and the pervasiveness of the smoke, there was much *damage* done and the family settled with the insurance company. As bad as it was, it could have been worse. They could have lost a family member — but they didn't.

Just as the young man knew that when he called 911 he would get help, so we too can pray to God in times of distress and know that He will answer us. God will answer our prayers of distress. The Psalmist in Psalm 118:5 (a psalm of thankfulness) writes, *"I called upon the Lord in distress: the Lord answered me, and set me in a large place."*

Now, it is interesting to note that the Psalmist does not state what kind of distress this is. It could be as small as a situation my wife and daughter have found themselves in on a number of different occasions. They would be ready, have the car loaded, and have everything they needed except the keys. They would get frustrated and go on the big hunt trying to remember where they left the keys. Then, after five or ten minutes, my wife would say to my daughter, "We need to ask Jesus to help us find the keys." They would pray, and soon thereafter they would find the keys. It occasionally became comical to my wife because sometimes it was my daughter who would speak up first and say, "We need to ask Jesus to help us find the keys, don't we, Mommy?" He always helped them.

We could also find ourselves in a very highly distressful circumstance, such as when I was home from college one summer. I remember walking into the kitchen to ask my 83-year-old grandma a question while she was talking to my uncle on the phone. All of a sudden, in mid-sentence, her body started convulsing; she lost her ability to speak; and her eyes rolled back in her head. She was having a seizure. I immediately took the phone from her hand, told my uncle to come quickly (he lived 10 minutes away), and called 911. They told me to take her out of her chair and lay her on her side until the paramedics arrived. This was a very difficult situation for me because it was the first time I had ever seen someone have a seizure. That was ten years ago. Today my grandmother is still alive and walking with God.

We do not know what kind of distress we may find ourselves in, but we can say with the Psalmist, "I called upon the Lord in distress and the Lord answered me."

We have Past Problems

All of us have had difficulties in the past. What did you do in the middle of that problem? Did you call on the name of the Lord? If so, you will be able to agree with the Psalmist as we continue to probe into this verse. Now, as we notice different aspects about this verse, the word "called" is in the past tense. This activity of calling upon the name of the Lord in distress had already taken place. The Psalmist had called upon God when he had been in distress and God had answered him. God was real to him. How about you, believer? Do you have a past record of calling upon the name of the Lord in your distress? Are you assured that God hears and answers your prayers? You can be.

I once had a mother speak to me about her 19-year-old son's prayer life. His father and she had encouraged him to pray, and he told them he did not pray because God did not hear his prayers. On one specific occasion, the young man was sick and had a high fever. On a Wednesday night the parents requested prayer for him and we prayed for him that same night as a church. His parents then went home and encouraged him to pray, and he did. By Sunday the fever was gone; he was back to good health, and he had received confidence in his prayer life. What happened, you ask? He prayed. He called upon the name of the Lord in his distress. When I saw the family on Sunday, they all just beamed with excitement at what the Lord had done.

Do you have this same confidence that you can call upon the name of the Lord in distress and God will hear and answer you? God had this past record with the Psalmist; He has it with many others of his children, and He wants to have it with you. You may be going through a distressing situation *right now*. Begin your prayer record with God by calling upon the name of the Lord. He wants to answer you and He will. If you still have unsolved problems from your past, call upon the name of the Lord; He will also solve your problems.

We Have Painful Problems

We need to call upon the name of the Lord when we have painful problems. As we look further at Psalm 118:5, we notice that the word "distress" means a "predicament or painful situation." The following story was told by Dr. Helen Roseveare, missionary to Zaire:

> "A mother at our mission station died after giving birth to a premature baby. We tried to improvise an incubator to keep the infant alive, but the only hot water bottle we had was beyond repair. So we asked the children to pray for the baby and for her sister. One of the girls responded, 'Dear God, please send a hot water bottle today. Tomorrow will be too late because by then the baby will be dead. And dear Lord, send a doll for the sister so she won't feel so lonely.'
>
> "That afternoon a large package arrived from England. The children watched eagerly as we opened it. Much to their surprise, under some clothing was a hot water bottle! Immediately the girl who had prayed so earnestly started to dig deeper, exclaiming, 'If God sent that, I'm sure He also sent a doll!' And she was right! The heavenly Father knew in advance of that child's sincere requests, and five months earlier He had led a ladies' group to include both of those specific articles."[1]

This situation on the mission field was very distressing to the little girl who had called on the name of the Lord that day. I'm sure that you have circumstances in your life that distress you. Do you call upon the name of the Lord in these times? He wants to answer your prayers too. We need to call upon the name of the Lord when we have painful problems.

God Pays Attention to our Problems

When we call upon the name of the Lord, God pays attention to our problems. Another important word in this verse, and one that captures our attention, is the word "answered." This word conveys the meaning "to heed, to respond, to give answer, or to pay attention." We see here that God paid attention to the prayer of the Psalmist, and He desires to give answer to your request when you call upon His name in a time of distress. Sometimes we are distressed about our own circumstances and sometimes we are distressed about the circumstances of others. In a book on the life of the late Jonathan Goforth, missionary to China in the late 1800's, the following story is related:

"When Mr. Goforth was preaching in the chapel, the Chinese men often pointed to Mr. McGillivray, saying, 'You speak, we don't understand him,' pointing to Goforth.

"Then, in God's own mysterious way, he performed one of His wonders in answer to prayer. One day as Jonathan was about to leave for the chapel, he said to his wife, 'If the Lord does not work a miracle for me with this language, I fear I will be an utter failure as a missionary!' For a moment he looked at the heartbreak that that would mean. Then picking up his Bible, he started off. Two hours later, he returned.

" 'Oh, Rose!' he cried, 'It was just wonderful! When I began to speak, those phrases and idioms that would always elude me came readily. The men actually asked me to go on though Donald had risen to speak. I *know* the backbone of the language is broken! Praise the Lord!' About two months later, a letter came from Mr. Talling (his former roommate, still in Knox), saying that on a certain evening after supper, a number of students decided to meet in one of the classrooms for prayer, 'just for Goforth.' The letter stated that the presence and power of God was so clearly felt by all at that meeting, they were convinced Goforth must surely have been helped in some way. On looking in his diary, Mr. Goforth found the students' prayer meeting in Knox coincided with the experience recorded above."[2]

Just as God prompted those students in that prayer meeting to pray for Jonathan Goforth, knowing that his faith as a preacher was in a distressed situation, so God *also* wants to prompt us to pray for others in distressing situations, too. The next time God lays someone upon your heart in a very distinct way, and you can't get them out of your mind, pray for them. Pray earnestly for them; for when we call upon His name, God pays attention to our problems.

God plentifully solves our problems

When we call upon the name of the Lord, He will plentifully solve our problems. Probably the most *exciting reason* about calling upon the name of the Lord in a distressing time is found in the last part of this verse. It states that, "the Lord answered me, and set me in a large place." This two-word phrase, "large place" (as is noted by Spurgeon), can also be rendered, "The Lord answered me largely." God will not only answer our prayers, but He will answer our prayers in a large way. He will answer them in ways we cannot foresee or even think to ask. Solomon, as he assumed the throne of Israel as a young man, prayed and simply asked God for wisdom. That is all; nothing more. Would you have been distressed, as a young man in your twenties, to be taking the throne of a nation of millions of people? I am sure I would be, and Solomon was, too. Yet, when he called upon the name of the Lord in his distressing situation, he simply asked for an understanding heart to rule God's people. God answered his prayer, and He did it in a large way. God responded to his prayer in I Kings 3:11-14, which states:

"Because thou hast asked this thing, and hast not asked for thyself long life; neither hast asked riches for thyself, nor hath asked the life of thine enemies; but hast

asked for thyself understanding to discern judgment; Behold, I have done according to thy words: lo, I have given thee a wise and an understanding heart; so that there was none like thee before thee, neither after thee shall any arise like unto thee. And I have also given thee that which thou hast not asked, both riches, and honour: so that there shall not be any among the kings like unto thee all thy days. And if thou wilt walk in my ways, to keep my statutes and my commandments, as thy father David did walk, then I will lengthen thy days."

How exciting, how wonderful, how tremendous our God is when He answers our prayers. He always answers us when we call upon His name in a time of distress, and He will answer us in a large way.

I'm reminded of the following story which should encourage your faith.

"While crossing the Atlantic on an oceanliner, F.B. Meyer was asked to address the first-class passengers. At the captain's request he spoke on 'Answered prayer.' An agnostic who was present at the service was asked by his friends, 'What did you think of Dr. Meyer's sermon?' He answered, 'I didn't believe a word of it.' That afternoon Meyer went to speak to a group of passengers. Many of the listeners at his morning address went along, including the agnostic, who claimed he just wanted to hear 'what the babbler had to say.'

"Before starting for the service, the agnostic put two oranges in his pocket. On his way he passed an elderly woman sitting in her deck chair fast asleep. Her hands were open. In the spirit of fun, the agnostic put the two oranges in her outstretched palms. After the meeting, he saw the old lady happily eating one of the pieces of fruit. 'You seem to be enjoying that orange,' he remarked with a smile. 'Yes, sir,' she replied, 'My Father is very good to me.' 'Your father? Surely your father can't be still alive!' 'Praise God,' she replied, 'He is very much alive.' 'What do you mean?' pressed the agnostic. She explained, 'I'll tell you, sir. I have been seasick for days. I was asking God somehow to send me an orange. I suppose I fell asleep while I was praying. When I awoke, I found He had not only sent me one orange but two!' The agnostic was speechless. Later he was converted to Christ. Yes, praying in God's will brings an answer."[3]

God wants us to call upon His name in times of distress just as this lady did who was in need of an orange. God will answer us. He will answer us greatly.

Believer, are you going through a time of distress in some personal area of your life? Is there something happening? Are the circumstances of life driving you to the conclusion that only prayer can help? Then it is time for you to call upon the name of the Lord in your distress. He will answer you just as He answered the Psalmist and other of His saints. God plentifully solves our problems.

Commitment Prayer

Heavenly Father, I cannot hide anything from you because you are sovereign. I come to you in my own personal distressing situation and I'm asking you to give attention to my heart's request and answer me. Father, just as you answered the Psalmist in a great way, I'm trusting you that you will do the same in my life. Thank you, Lord, for answers to my prayers in the past. In Jesus' name, amen.

[1] Internet site: www.bible.org.

[2] Goforth, Rosalind. *Jonathan Goforth* (Minneapolis, MN: Bethany House Publishers, 1986), p. 49.

[3] Internet site: www.bible.org.

When We Call Upon God, He Will Draw Nigh to Us

"The Lord is nigh unto all that call upon him, to all that call upon him in truth."
                                           Psalm 145:18

SIR ISAAC NEWTON said that he could take his telescope and look millions and millions of miles into space. Then he added, "But when I lay it aside, go into my room, shut the door, and get down on my knees in earnest prayer, I see more of heaven and feel closer to the Lord than if I were assisted by all the telescopes on earth."[1]

We all have times in our lives when we feel closer to God than at others. Psalm 145:18 states, *"The Lord is nigh unto all that call upon him, to all that call upon him in truth."* We know that the Holy Spirit indwells us from the point of salvation. We know that God is omnipresent. God is everywhere at all times. We know that God is omniscient and knows our every thought even before we think it. Yet there seem to be times when we, as the children of God, feel farther from Him than at others. This brings us back to the importance of calling upon the name of the Lord. Our prayer time is vitally important to our closeness to God. E.M. Bounds said,

What the church needs today is not more or better machinery, not new organizations or more and novel methods, but men whom the Holy Ghost can use — men of prayer, men mighty in prayer. The Holy Ghost does not flow through methods but through men. He does not come on machinery, but on men. He does not anoint plans but men — men of prayer."

In essence, E.M. Bounds is saying the same as Psalm 145:18, *"The Lord is nigh unto all that call upon Him, to all that call upon Him in truth."*

There are two facets of calling upon the name of the Lord in this verse that arrest our attention: (1) God approaches us when we call upon Him, and (2) We can be assured of His presence when we call upon Him. God is at hand when we call upon His name. Here in Psalm 145:18, the word "nigh" implies nearness (as in place, kindred, or time), to align oneself with, to approach, or to be at hand. The psalmist is saying that we can count on God to approach us and to be at hand when we call upon His name.

When we consider this, the Old Testament prophet Jeremiah comes to mind. Jeremiah, the weeping prophet, was a man of compassion called to give a hard message to the nation of Israel in a time when Israel had turned back on God. He was called to announce to Israel that when Babylon came up against them, they were to just give up because they were going to lose the battle. God had said so. It wasn't that Jeremiah was not patriotic; just the opposite. He remained single at this time in his life so God could use his life message to present a living example of God's truth to the Jews. Jeremiah was a devoted patriot, wholly committed to God and to holiness. He was faithful over the course of twenty-plus years to prophesy to Israel impending judgment, without ever having one convert. He compassionately warned the Jews that if they did not repent, their prize city, Jerusalem would be destroyed. Much of Jeremiah's ministry had to do with sharing with his fellow Israelites that their oppression and coming defeat by Babylon were God's way of calling them to repentance and faith. Sometimes known as "the prophet of doom," he had few friends and many enemies. On one occasion he even decided that he would stop prophesying for God. Yet when he did this, he said he could not keep silent for long because God's Word was as a fire shut up in his bones. He had to be God's mouthpiece; he could not keep silent.

Jeremiah had natural concerns for his nation. He was by birth a priest; yet was chosen and called before his birth to be a prophet (Jeremiah 1:5). His ministry followed on the heels of a time of revival in Israel's history, yet during his ministry his nation was in a time of spiritual recession. Despite his faithful care, compassion, concern, and uncompromising message for Israel, Jeremiah and his message from God were rejected by Israel. He was accused of being a traitor and was imprisoned five times. Tradition tells us that after Babylon overthrew Jerusalem and took most of the people captive, Jeremiah was left with a remnant who (due to famine) retreated to Egypt and later stoned Jeremiah to death.

In Jeremiah 38 we find one of the low points in the life of Jeremiah. In verse 4 the princes of the city request King Zedekiah to put Jeremiah to death. He tells them that he will not stop them if they wish to do so. Jeremiah 38:4-6 reads,

"Therefore the princes said unto the king, We beseech thee, let this man be put to death: for thus he weakeneth the hands of the men of war that remain in this city, and the hands of all the people, in speaking such words unto them: for this man seeketh not the welfare of this people, but the hurt. Then Zedekiah the king said, Behold, he is in your hand: for the king is not he that can do any thing against you."

These men who wished to kill Jeremiah for his bold proclamations of the truth took him to prison and put him in a dungeon. This was not simply a damp cellar-type dungeon like the one in which he had been placed in Chapter 37 (after having been beaten according to the Jewish tradition: forty stripes save one). This dungeon had a *pit* of mire. The *pit* was so deep that they had to let him down with cords; and was probably an old well since the writer takes pains to note that there was no water in this pit — just mire. Jeremiah's body sunk down into the mire. Then, after they let him down into the *pit*, his captors threw a stone into the *pit* hoping to hit him on the head and take his life. How many days he was there is not described for us, yet we know this was not kept secret. An Ethiopian servant of King Zedekiah, named Ebedmelech, heard what had happened to Jeremiah and became so concerned for Jeremiah's life that he went to the King and requested permission to rescue Jeremiah. The king granted his request and gave him charge of thirty men to help in the rescue. Thus Jeremiah was rescued from the miry *pit*.

In another book of the Bible, Jeremiah recorded his personal conversation with God in the midst of horrible circumstances. Lamentations 3:55-57 reads, *"I called upon thy name, O Lord, out of the low dungeon. Thou hast heard my voice; hide not thine ear at my breathing, at my cry."*

This man of God had a personal walk with God. He had a real prayer life. In the midst of this life-and-death circumstance, he cried out to God. He called upon the name of the Lord and the Lord heard his voice; even his breath, Jeremiah says. We see the key to the answering of Jeremiah's prayer in verse 57, "Thou drewest near to me in the day that I called upon thee; thou saidst, Fear not." Jeremiah, in the dire situation in which he found himself, personally received a message from God (not for a nation but for himself). Imagine how you would feel in his circumstances. What thoughts might go through your mind? What emotions might run through your body? Perhaps you would have thoughts and feelings of abandonment, even rejection in its highest form. Yet, God heard his prayer and answered him with just what he needed to hear, "Fear not." God loves us. He wants us, as His dear children, to call upon His name. He will draw nigh to us; He will hear our cry to Him; He will answer our prayers; He will meet our needs. Here is a prophet of God with whom many of us can empathize. However, we must know that God is alive; that He is actively in charge; that He is still on His throne. Cry out to Him; call upon His name. He will draw nigh to you. He will align Himself with you against your enemies when He approaches you. He will answer your prayers. D.L. Moody said, "It is a great thing to have a place of resort in a time of trouble ... to think, when the heart is burdened, we can go and pour it into His ear, and then have the answer come back, 'I will be with you.' There is comfort in that!"[2]

The second important teaching of this verse is that when we call upon the name of the Lord, we must do so in truth. *"The Lord is nigh unto all them that call upon Him, to all that call upon Him in truth."* When we call upon the Lord and we desire for Him to draw nigh unto us, we must call upon Him in truth: it cannot simply be an emotion or thought. There are two types of truth: factual truth, and perceived (either mentally thought or emotionally felt) truth. Factual truth is real life circumstance, coming to God and stating the facts just as they are. Perceived truth may not be the actual facts in a given situation but may seem very real to us. However, only one of these types of truth is real. The other is not. For instance, you might have a series of events happen at work where you get called into your boss's office and reprimanded for something that happened on the worksite whether or not it was your fault. About the fourth or fifth time that you get called in you *may* be fearful that you are about to be fired. Your mind thinks, "What could I have done now?" Your heart is racing as you walk to his office. Sweat beads start to form on your forehead. You just know that you are about to get fired. Then you open his door and walk in. He greets you and asks you to sit down. He is quiet and sort of serious, looking over papers in his hands. "He is reviewing my records," you think. As you sit down, he says, "I've been reviewing the incidents of the past two weeks and have found that they were not your fault at all but ...." Then he gives some easily understood explanations. He says to you, "Actually, I am quite happy with how you've responded to each of our previous meetings and I am going to recommend you for a better job with better benefits in another area of our company." Inside you think, "Wow! That was a close call!" But was it really? No. You just thought it was.

When we call upon God and desire Him to draw near to us, we need to do so in truth. This word "truth" has the meaning of stability, certainty, trustworthiness, or faithfulness. God wants us to call upon His name with complete faith and confidence that we can rest assured in Him. We can be assured that He will draw nigh to us; that He is in control. No matter what circumstances we find ourselves in, we must call upon His name in truth. Jeremiah's situation was a genuine life and death situation. When He called upon the name of the Lord, the Lord drew near to him and answered his prayer. God wants you and me to call upon His name in truth also. He will draw nigh to us and answer our prayers.

Commitment Prayer

Heavenly Father, I confess that sometimes when I pray to you it is not with complete faith and confidence in you, and sometimes I do not have all the facts. Please forgive me for those times when I lack faith or knowledge and cry out emotionally, not genuinely resting assured that you will draw near and answer my prayer. I desire to call upon your name in truth and to confidently trust you to be near me and to answer my prayer. In Jesus' name, amen.

[1] Internet site: www.bible.org.

[2] Paxton, Sam. *Short Quotations of D.L. Moody*, (Chicago, IL: Moody Press, 1961), p. 43.

We Need to Call Upon God Daily

*"Because he hath inclined his ear unto me,
therefore will I call upon him as long as I live."*
Psalm 116:2

THE STORY is told of George Mueller's answered prayers on behalf of his friends. He personally prayed for the salvation of five of his friends. After five years, one of them came to Christ. In ten years, two more of them found peace in the same Savior. He prayed on for 25 years, and the fourth man was saved. For the fifth, George Mueller prayed until the time of his death; and then this friend, too, came to Christ a few months after Mr. Mueller went on to heaven. For this latter friend, Mr. Mueller had prayed almost 52 years.[1]

What compelled George Mueller to keep praying for the salvation of the fifth friend? God had answered his prayers in the past. This is similar to what the Psalmist wrote in Psalm 116:2, *"Because he hath inclined his ear unto me, therefore will I call upon him as long as I live."* The Psalmist could point to prior occasions when he had prayed to God and received answers: when he called on God, God heard his prayer and answered it.

Concerning his time alone with God, Eric Liddell (the renown Scottish athlete, immortalized in *Chariots of Fire*, who later became a missionary to China) confided in some friends that each morning he set aside some time to meditate and pray or read some passage from the Bible. This was his special time with God which helped him to plan his entire day. And if circumstances sometimes forced him to miss that time with His Maker, he felt at odds with the world and everyone in it for the rest of that day. It was as if he was "out of tune" with God Himself.[2] I know exactly how Eric felt after not spending his daily time alone with God. I have felt the same way, too. Doesn't it seem like we are out of step with the rest of our day when we miss our time with God? He should be first every day.

We need to call upon God *daily* in prayer. In 1991, God afforded me the opportunity to go to Haiti and preach in some churches. These churches had been started by a man who had grown up as an adopted young man in my grandparents' home when they were missionaries to Haiti. He got saved; God called him to preach; and he began doing the work of God. One of the most precious memories to me from my trip was the daily prayer time this man had with his church leadership. Every morning from 5:30 a.m. to 6:30 a.m., six or seven men would gather at his house for a time of prayer. I had the opportunity to join their prayer meetings while I was there. Although I didn't understand most of the men who prayed because they were praying in French Creole, I could understand that they were communing with God and that He was meeting with us. What a blessing and encouragement it was to me to see these men daily meeting for prayer on behalf of their church and their community.

Calling upon the name of the Lord *daily* takes discipline. A believer must truly be committed to God and deem the fellowship necessary to their *daily* duties. John Wesley was known for rising each day at 4:00 a.m. to spend time alone with God in prayer. Martin Luther, the great Reformer, said, "I have so much to do that I cannot get on without three hours a day of prayer." How about you, Christian? Are you disciplined and habitually spending time calling upon the name of the Lord? The truth is, until prayer becomes an intricate part of your walk with God, you will not be a consistent believer. You will be a hit-and-miss Christian. You will lack genuine commitment in your walk with God, your spiritual growth, and your consistent testimony before other believers. When you begin calling on the name of the Lord *daily*, you will enlarge your sphere of influence in this world as salt and light for the kingdom of God.

Robert E. Lee, the famous general of the confederate army in the civil war was also known to be a man of prayer. He had his regular hours of secret devotion during which he allowed nothing else, however pressing, to interrupt. He neglected no opportunity of joining in the public devotions of God's people. Chaplain Jones said: "I saw him frequently at our services in the army, as he listened with moistened eyes to the truths of the gospel, or bowed in the dust as some one led the devotions of the congregation." General Lee always had his family altar and read family prayers every morning just before breakfast. A daughter-in-law, after her first visit to General Lee, spending three weeks in his home, said that she did not believe he would have an entirely high opinion of any person, even General Washington, if he could return to earth, if he were not in time for family prayers.[3]

The phrase that we find at the end of Psalm 116:2 is an important one. In our English Bibles we read, *"Because he hath inclined his ear unto me, therefore will I call upon him as long as I live."* The Hebrew expression used here is "yowm yowm." "Yowm" is the word for day. We could interpret it as "day by day," "as long as I live," or "year to year." These are the different ways that we find it translated in our English Bible. It would mean, in essence, "daily". Daily accomplishing a task speaks of commitment.

Some years ago a man in our church retired from a company for whom he had faithfully worked for 30 years. At the end of those 30 years nearly everyone of his fellow employees attended a party held in his honor, attesting to his loyalty and years of service. He had been faithful in his *commitment* to the company. He had a *commitment* to his company. This is commitment here on earth, what about our heavenly commitment? Christian, how is your daily prayer *commitment* to God? Is it a brief conversation you have with God similar to one you might have with a long distance friend? You can't afford to talk to them daily so you talk to them weekly. For all of the activities that you are involved in, do you spend time daily with God in prayer? If not, begin today. Ask God's Holy Spirit to remind you each day when you wake up to spend time with your Heavenly Father in prayer.

And what of your commitment to God — Are you close to Him? Is he close to you? Abraham was called the friend of God; the Bible says, *"Enoch walked with God."* In Genesis 39, we find the story that speaks expressly of Joseph's dedication. He was hated by his brothers, ousted from his family, sold into slavery to foreigners, taken to another country, and purchased as a common household servant by Potiphar. The Bible further tells us that Joseph was *committed* to excellence and that Potiphar placed all he had under Joseph's authority; everything, that is, except his wife. Genesis 39:7 states, *"And it came to pass after these things, that his master's wife cast her eyes upon Joseph; and she said, Lie with me."* Joseph, however said to Potiphar's wife, "How then can I do this great wickedness, and sin against God?" He recognized that the most important relationship he had in life was his relationship with God; walking with God was his priority. It is interesting to note the phrase, "day by day" in verse 10. Every day Potiphar's wife came after Joseph; tempting him, enticing him to commit sin. Yet *every day* he kept his *commitment* to God. He hearkened not to her, neither to lie by her nor to be with her. He had such strong *daily devotion* to God that it kept him from sin though it eventually cost him his position. How strong is your relationship with God, Christian? Are you falling into the same trap laid by the enemy in your path? Do you forget to have your *daily* prayer time with God? *Daily* speaks of the importance of the *commitment* we have to God.

Another situation in Scripture where we find this Hebrew expression *day by day* is Exodus 29:38 and Numbers 28:3,4. In Exodus 29:38-39, God is giving instructions to Moses concerning the offering of sacrificial lambs when he states, *"Now this is that which thou shalt offer upon the altar; two lambs of the first year day by day continually. The one lamb thou shalt offer in the morning; and the other lamb thou shalt offer at even."* These instructions are repeated again for us in Numbers 28:3,4, reading, *"This is the offering made by fire which ye shall offer unto the Lord: two lambs of the first year without spot day by day, for a continual burnt offering. The one lamb shalt thou offer in the morning, and the other lamb shalt thou offer at even."*

In both places of Scripture we find the phrase "day by day." This phrase is the same Hebrew phrase that we read in Psalm 116:2, "as long as I live." Here in the Exodus and Numbers passages, these verses refer to a daily sacrifice of a lamb as a perpetual atonement for the people of Israel. God was exact in ordering from the Israelites what he desired. He wanted only the best lambs sacrificed to Him morning and evening, continually. This *sacrifice* and burnt offering was not only on behalf of the people but it was also a form of worship. These lambs did not purge, cover, or atone for the sins of Israel but were only a picture or type of the Lamb of God that was to be slain: the shedding of His blood (individually accepted) takes away the sins of the whole world. Yet God was still meticulous in His requirements of Israel.

Again, we see God desiring from his people a strong *commitment* to worship Him; and when we call upon the name of the Lord daily, we are committed to Him. How strong is your personal *commitment* to the Lord? Christian, you need to be calling on the name of the Lord daily. You should not make an excuse for not spending time with God in prayer. Give God the best part of your day. Promise Him or pledge that you will call upon Him in the morning when you first rise and in the evening as you turn in: sacrificially give God your time in daily worship.

Commitment Prayer

Heavenly Father, thank you so much for the privilege of prayer. Please forgive me for not being disciplined in my prayer time and calling upon Your name daily. May Your Holy Spirit remind me of God's grace to me on a daily basis and my need to call on You. I commit to You the first fruits of my day in spending time with You. In Jesus' name, amen.

---

[1] Tan, Paul Lee. *Encyclopedia of 15,000 Illustrations* (Dallas, TX: Bible Communications, 1998), 2193.

[2] Swift, Catherine. *Eric Liddell* (Minneapolis, MN: Bethany House, 1990), 81.

[3] Johnson, William J. *Robert E. Lee The Christian* (Milford, MI: Mott Media, 1976), 205-206.

8

We Must Praise the Lord When We Call upon Him

"I will call upon the Lord, who is worthy to be praised: so shall I be saved from mine enemies."

Psalm 18:3

DAVID ANOINTED, but not yet crowned king, had been on the run from King Saul for about seven years when news came to him that Saul had died in battle against the Philistines. Upon receiving this news, David sat down and penned the words to Psalm 18. The introduction reads,

> To the chief Musician, A Psalm of David, the servant of the Lord, who spake unto the Lord the words of this song in the day that the Lord delivered him from the hand of all his enemies, and from the hand of Saul.

I imagine that, for David, those years after having been anointed the next king over Israel were very turbulent, with multiple mountain-top and valley experiences. On many different occasions King Saul tried to take David's life, sometimes by his own hand and sometimes by the hand of his soldiers. There were even a couple of occasions when David was so close to Saul that David could have thrust him through with his own sword. Yet, we find that David was not willing to lift his hand against the Lord's anointed. It is upon this day, the day of Saul's death, that David penned the words of Psalm 18:3, which reads, *"I will call upon the Lord, who is worthy to be praised: so shall I be saved from mine enemies."* David had a reason to praise God when he called upon his name — God had saved him or delivered him from his enemies, even his chief enemy, King Saul. We, too, need to recognize that when we call upon the name of the Lord, we should praise Him for what He has accomplished in our lives. When we do praise God in this manner, we will find personal intimacy and wonderful excitement as we extol the King of Glory on our knees in prayer. We will also be more readily able to identify with King David's words, *"I will call upon the Lord, who is worthy to be praised."*

So how can we praise the Lord upon whose name we are calling? Isaiah 12:4 states, *"And in that day shall we say, Praise the Lord, call upon his name, declare his doing among the people, make mention that His name is exalted."* Here in this verse we find two ways that we may praise God while calling upon His name: (1) Declare his doing and (2) Make mention that his name is exalted.

If we are truly going to praise the Lord, or be thankful for what He has done, then we must declare his doings. The word "declare" carries with it the idea of being aware or acknowledging. If we are going to declare God's doings in our lives, we must be able to comprehend what His doings are. We must be aware of His working and be able to acknowledge His hand in our lives.

I recall the story of a medical missionary who was home on furlough declaring one of God's doings in his life:

> While serving at a small field hospital in Africa, I traveled every two weeks by bicycle through the jungle to a nearby city for supplies. This required camping overnight halfway. On one of these trips, I saw two men

fighting in the city. One was seriously injured, so I treated him and witnessed to him of the Lord Jesus Christ. I then returned home without incident.

Upon arriving in the city several weeks later, I was approached by the man I had treated earlier. He told me he had known that I carried money and medicine. He said, 'Some friends and I followed you into the jungle knowing you would camp overnight. We waited for you to sleep and planned to kill you and take your money and drugs. Just as we were about to move into your campsite, we saw that you were surrounded by 26 armed guards.'

I laughed at this and said I was certainly all alone out in that jungle campsite. The young man pressed the point, "No, sir, I was not the only one to see the guards. My friends also saw them and we all counted them. It was because of those guards that we were afraid and left you alone.

At this point in the church presentation in Michigan, one of the men in the church jumped up and interrupted the missionary, and asked, 'Can you tell me the exact date when this happened?' The missionary thought for a while and recalled the date. The man in the congregation told this side of the story:

On that night in Africa it was morning here. I was preparing to play golf. As I put my bag in the car, I felt the Lord leading me to pray for you. In fact, the urging was so strong that I called the men of this church together to pray for you. Will all of those men who met with me that day please stand?'

The men who had met that day to pray together stood — there were 26 of them![1]

What an exciting time those people in that church must have had in that church service. One man declared the doings of our God while another reminded the church that twenty-six men were calling on the name of the Lord on the missionary's behalf.

If we are going to praise the Lord, we must also make mention that He is exalted. The word "mention" here has the understanding of "to remember, to be mindful, make to be remembered, call to remembrance, and in some cases to think on." As we call upon the name of the Lord, we must remind ourselves who God is and where He is. He is exalted. This word "exalted" can mean "to set up on high, to be set on high, to make lofty or excellent." Too often when we call upon the name of the Lord, we try to bring God down to man's level, within man's reach. Yet our great God, the one whom we desire to hear from, is exalted. He is set on the high throne of the universe. He is the Creator of all. He reigns over all. He is the Lofty One of Israel, and we are but His servants. When we call upon Him, we must praise Him. We must confess His greatness before Him. D.L. Moody once said,

> Every good gift that we have had from the cradle up has come from God. If a man just stops to think what he has to praise God for, he will find there is enough to keep him singing His praises for a week.[2]

Fellow believer, when you call on the name of the Lord, are you in the habit of praising our great God? Do you take time to declare His mighty doings to Him in prayer and to others in public? Are you in the habit of being forgetful or having short-term memory on the answers of God to your prayers because you have so much more you desire to ask of him? Take time to declare His doings. Take time to make mention that He is exalted. Our God is set upon high. He alone is thoroughly excellent. Christian, when you pray (when you call upon the name of the Lord), praise Him; He is worthy to be praised!

Commitment Prayer

Heavenly Father, I must confess that in my prayers recently I have neglected to praise You. You are doing great deeds in my life; but I have not made mention that you are exalted in either my private prayers or my public conversations. Please forgive me for this and remind me on a regular basis that "daily you load me with benefits," and that daily I should praise your name! In Jesus' name, amen.

---

[1] Although I had heard this story on different occasions I found the details at www.bible.org.

[2] Paxton, Sam. *Short Quotations of D. L. Moody*, (Chicago, IL: Moody Press, 1961), 42.

9

When We Call Upon God, It Will Influence our Worship

"I will offer to thee the sacrifice of thanksgiving, and will call upon the name of the LORD."
Psalm 116:17

WHEN A PERSON or group of people call upon the name of the Lord, their worship will be influenced. C.H. Spurgeon once said:

> The condition of the church may be very accurately gauged by its prayer meetings. So is the prayer meeting a grace-ometer, and from it we may judge the amount of divine working among people. If God be near a church, it must pray. And if He be not there, one of the first tokens of His absence will be slothfulness in prayer.[1]

Charles Spurgeon and his church believed in practicing prayer, and they saw it greatly influence their worship. The story is told of two men who went to visit the Tabernacle to hear Spurgeon preach. As usual, when they arrived early, before the doors to the great hall opened, they found a line forming, yet they were very near the front. They were excited to be there and wanted to take a tour before church, if possible; so they began knocking on the door. To their satisfaction, someone answered the door, and after they explained that they had traveled a distance, the person agreed to bring them in and give them a tour. The man took them through the large auditorium and back through the offices, describing many wonderful aspects of the ministry. Near the end of the tour, the guide said to the two men as they approached some stairs to the basement, "Let me show you our heater room." At first the two men looked at each other, thinking this a little odd. Yet, they had come this far, so why not continue? As they went down the stairs and through the hallway, they came to a door of a room that was closed. The guide quietly opened the door, and the two visitors then realized what he had meant by "heater room." In the room, they found 400 believers fervently praying for the services nigh at hand. Their guide, they later discovered, was none other than C.H. Spurgeon himself.

When we call upon the name of the Lord, both personally and corporately, it will influence our worship. We will know our worship has affected us not only by how our lives are effected on Sunday, but during the week as well. In this chapter we will consider three men whose worship was impacted by their calling on the name of the Lord: Abraham, Isaac, and David.

Abraham's Worship Influenced His Wandering

In Genesis 12 God told Abraham to leave his home land, Ur of the Chaldees, to go to a land that He would later show him. Abraham's obedience was a step of faith, displaying his trust in Jehovah. Abraham was 75 years old when he left Haran. Journeying from Haran into the land of Canaan, he came to a place called Shechem. As he passed through this land, the Lord again appeared unto him. This time the Lord was confirming that Canaan was the land that He would give to Abraham's seed. Prior to this, when the Lord told Abraham to move, Abraham had gone with little knowledge of where, when, or how he would reach his destination. However, here in Genesis 12, God appeared to Abraham and gave him clearer directions: God said to Abraham, "This is the land." (Before the land of Canaan on this side of Jordan was promised to the Israelites who fled Egypt, it was promised to Abraham.)

It was at this point in time that God showed him the where, but not the when or the how. Abraham's blind, faithful obedience to the will of God brought him that much closer to the completion of the will of God. However, there was one small problem, posed as a simple statement at the end of verse 6, "And the Canaanite was then in the land." Canaan was the where, and before Abraham died, God even showed him the when; but he never told Abraham the how. Abraham was simply a wanderer through the land at this time; if he had been aware that God was going to use his descendants to annihilate the Canaanites he might have been tempted to get ahead of God's timing, stop being a wanderer, and become a warrior. He might have tried to do the job the Israelites were going to need to do at a later time.

Abraham was wandering through the land of Canaan when God appeared to him and confirmed the where. This reminds me of my missionary friends to Mexico, Mark and Cindy Ernst. They were surrendered to God, working as youth pastor in a church, when the person designated to lead a missions trip became ill. Mark and Cindy were asked to fill in, and while they were on that trip, they "wandered" through a town outside of Saltillo called Arteaga. They then stopped in Arteaga, and God impressed upon their hearts the need in that town for a gospel preaching missionary and confirmed in their hearts that this was the place in which He wanted them to serve. That was almost ten years ago; God has done a wonderful work through their lives there in Arteaga and continues to do so today.

When God appeared to Abraham in verse 7, Abraham

stopped his wandering to take time out to worship Him. In verse 8 we see that Abraham stopped, pitched his tent, built an altar and called upon the name of the Lord. After this special time, he then journeyed southward. When Abraham called upon the name of the Lord, his worship affected his wandering.

Fellow believer, you might be wandering through some "detour" in your Christian life. You may be wandering (as Abraham did) by stepping out in faith, obeying some direction of the Lord. It may seem to have been a long while since you have heard from Him, but take time to call upon the name of the Lord. Verbally renew your faith and confidence in Him. Stop and build an altar to His glory. Reflect on where you have been in life and where He has brought you thus far; then trust Him to continue to lead until the journey is completed. Allow your worship to affect your wandering.

Isaac's Worship Influenced his Work

In Genesis 26, Isaac found himself in a most uncomfortable position. He was being blessed mightily of God, and this troubled his neighbors, the Philistines (especially Abimilech). They envied him. They had already gone through the land and filled in all of the wells that Abraham, Isaac's father, had dug. Now they saw the son prospering and becoming a mighty man among them, and they envied him so much they asked him to leave. When Isaac left the land of the Philistines, he removed from there and pitched his tents somewhere else in the land of Canaan and dug another well. When he did this, the herdsmen of Gerar strove with his herdsmen over the water that came from the well. So he let them have it and simply dug another well. They strove with him over this well, too; he moved again and dug another well. This time the herdsmen of Gerar left him alone and did not strive with him.

Not long after this Isaac went to Beersheba and the Lord appeared unto him and reconfirmed the Abrahamic blessing. This time God was concerned with telling Isaac about the gen-

generations to follow and how his seed would be multiplied. Now, the blessing was not only about the land but about the people as well. In the middle of all the moving that Isaac was doing, when God appeared to him, he stopped digging wells and built an altar and called upon the name of the Lord. Isaac's work had been affected by his worship. He had been sent out by the Philistines and they strove with him. The herdsmen of Gerar had striven with him over the wells. Neither group was happy with him because of the blessing that God had poured out on him. He then focused his fellowship towards heaven and called upon the name of the Lord. After Isaac called upon the name of the Lord, Abimelech and others came to make an oath with Isaac. God tells us in Proverbs 16:7, *"When a man's ways please the Lord, He maketh even his enemies to be at peace with him."* Isaac had enemies. Isaac built an altar and called upon the name of the Lord. His enemies came to make a covenant of peace with him. So he made them a feast and granted the covenant of peace they requested. That same day his servants found water and came to tell him.

Christian, how is your situation at work? Are you having difficulty with a fellow employee or maybe even a boss? Maybe you are having difficulty with a neighbor. Isaac stopped in the middle of all that he was doing and built an altar. He called upon the name of the Lord; he worshipped God. His worship of God affected his work with men. If you will take time to worship God and call upon the name of the Lord, perhaps your worship will affect your work too.

David's Worship Influenced his Wavering Faith

In I Chronicles 21, King David was tempted of Satan to number Israel. He was provoked to take his eyes of faith off of the Lord, who had led him to mighty victory after mighty victory, and to place them upon the number of soldiers that he had in his army. Joab, the captain of David's army, recognized this lack of faith and even counseled King David to forego this course of action. But David wanted the people numbered from the north to the south and from the east to the west. Even from Dan to Beersheba did David have the people of Israel numbered. Joab obeyed his king and gave King David the number of all the men of Israel who drew sword, an exorbitant amount of men, totaling up to one million, one hundred thousand soldiers. God had indeed greatly blessed David's military might. However, as is often the case with frail humans, David took his eyes off of the Blesser and focused on the blessing. Since David was the king of a great nation, and his faith in God and his walk with God were very important, this sin of David's (lack of faith in God) affected the whole nation of Israel in a devastating manner.

God sent Gad to tell King David that He was not pleased with David's numbering of the people, and that David could choose any one of three different pestilences that would be sent to Israel for David's sin. David chose the angel of the Lord to be sent to destroy throughout the land of Israel. God sent a mighty pestilence upon Israel, and 70,000 men died. The angel of the Lord was marching toward Israel to perform his work there when King David recognized that it was his lack of faith that brought this punishment upon the nation of Israel; therefore, he must be the one to repent before God. David's heart was convicted. His sin had been the cause of death in the lives of so many of his people that he cried out to God to be the one who received punishment, not the Israelites.

David then bought a piece of land, Ornan's threshing floor, so that he could build an altar to the Lord. I Chronicles 21:26 states:

And David built there an altar unto the Lord, and offered burnt offerings and peace offerings, and called upon the Lord; and he answered him from heaven by fire upon the altar of burn offering.

David called upon the Lord when he saw the results of his wavering faith. We are all responsible for our own faith in God and our walk with Him; yet, when we are in a position of authority, especially great authority, sometimes our decisions (right or wrong, good or bad), greatly affect the lives of those under our authority. Such was the case in I Chronicles. Yet when David repented, God responded. He answered from heaven. He answered with fire upon the altar in such a way that it was undeniably a response from God. David called upon the Lord and God heard and answered in a mighty way. Only God's Holy Spirit could have given the next entry in Scripture. I Chronicles 21:27 states, *"And the Lord commanded the angel; and he put up his sword again into the sheath thereof."* The plague of death had stopped. The pestilence had been stayed. When David called upon the Lord, his worship affected his wavering faith and the lives of so many people under his authority.

Christian, do not take your eyes off of the Almighty Blessing-Giver. Yes, He has blessed you in many ways with many things; but don't become so enamored with and enthralled by the blessings that you lose sight of Him. Don't boast in His blessings, but boast in the *Blesser*.

Call upon the name of the Lord. Worship Him. Allow your worship to affect your wandering as Abraham did. Allow your worship to influence your work as Isaac did. Allow your worship to impact your wavering faith as David did. My friend, call upon the name of the Lord and see God answer from heaven mightily on your behalf and bless you as His dear child.

Commitment Prayer

Heavenly Father, I come before you right now and I confess that I need to call upon your name concerning an area of my life. God, I have been wandering spiritually, and it has been a while since I have heard from you. I stop right here and take time out to build a spiritual altar and call upon your name. Please answer me and give me direction.

Lord, I can see the devastating effects of wavering faith in my life and in the lives of those around me. I choose to trust you with this area of my life that I have taken into my own hands. Please hear my prayer and answer me from heaven in a mighty way. In Jesus' name, amen.

---

[1] Carter, Tom. *2200 Quotations from the Writings of C. H. Spurgeon.* (Grand Rapids, MI: Baker Books, 1988), p. 155.

10

Praying for People
Instruction on Intercession

"I exhort therefore, that, first of all, supplications, prayers, intercessions, and giving of thanks, be made for all men."
1 Timothy 2:1

AS THE APOSTLE PAUL WROTE to a newer, younger minister for Christ, Timothy, he gave instructions on how to pray, and specifically how to pray for people. The four types of prayer that Paul said should be offered to God on behalf of men are: supplications (to make a request, petition or beg [as binding oneself]); prayers (a general word meaning to pray, or worship); intercessions (to deal with, to attain an object or a desired end); and thanksgivings (grateful language to God as an act of worship). Each of these types of prayers is an aspect of praying for people and interceding on their behalf, and each is necessary if the believer's prayer life is to make an impact on this world for eternity.

In this chapter the focus is, not on these four types individually, but on how they are a part of the broader picture of intercession. The two truths that will be emphasized in this chapter are: praying for people and the people for whom we should be praying.

Praying for People: Intercession

Its definition — As we consider the act of prayerfully interceding on behalf of another believer, we are reminded of the present work of the Savior as described in Romans 8:34, *"Who is he that condemneth? It is Christ that died, yea rather that is risen again, who is even at the right hand of God, who also maketh intercession for us."* Our Risen Lord and Savior (who has conquered death and hell and has ascended to be seated at the right hand of the Father) is presently interceding on our behalf. When we intercede in prayer on behalf of others, we are joining with Christ our Lord.

The word "intercession" supplies different facets through which our minds may view it. The dictionary defines intercession as, "to plead or to make a request on another's behalf." More specifically, the Greek word for intercession means, "a falling in with, pleading with God on another's behalf." The word picture painted for us here is that of a person purposefully falling into a ditch to help another who has fallen in and needs assistance getting out. A biblical example of this would be the good Samaritan. He saw that a Jewish man had fallen prey to thieves and had been beaten, robbed, and left for dead alongside the road. While the priest and the Levite did not even stop to see if the man was going to live, the Samaritan stopped, helped cleanse and wrap the man's wounds, and paid for him to stay in an inn until he was healed. The Samaritan was the one who interceded for the Jew in the biblical sense of the word. He involved himself in the Jew's circumstances with the intent and purpose of "helping him out of his ditch".

A modern day example of this compares to a person driving his automobile down the highway and noticing a car pulled off to the side of the road. As the driver draws closer to the car he realizes that the individual's car has a flat tire; and he pulls over and stops to help change it. Once he has helped the person with the flat tire he continues on his journey.

These word pictures describe intercessory prayer in the following way. When we become aware of someone's personal struggles or difficulties (whether spiritual, physical, or financial) we then start praying specifically for God to meet his needs. We will pray for him continually, daily, (often many times a day), until we see God answer our prayer request. Sometimes the answer comes quickly; other times it takes longer, as God is orchestrating more than one circumstance at a time. I started praying for my father's salvation on a regular, daily basis when I was sixteen-years-old. Eight years later, when I was twenty-four, my dad gave a clear testimony of accepting Christ as his Savior. I could see a difference in his life that evidenced the change too. For eight years I got into the ditch with my dad for an eternal change in the destiny of his soul. God had to work out many circumstances and situations, yet He answered my prayers when I interceded on behalf of my dad. All my other immediate family members had already given testimony of trusting Christ as their Savior; and now, with my father saved, I can expect to see my whole family in heaven.

Its duty — When we are interceding for someone in our private prayer place, our attitude toward them must be proper. It is our duty as believers to come to God in prayer, recognizing what our responsibility is and how we are to pray for an individual. In praying for a relational situation with a boss at work, you would need to recognize that he is a person in authority over you. It is not your responsibility to change him, either through your conduct or conversation at work nor through your prayers at home. You need to continually yield your boss and the situation over to the Lord, asking Him to do in this authority's life all that He desires to accomplish, and to continue to yield to that authority at work (unless of course there is some form of abuse occurring). Because you are a believer, it is your duty to intercede for your authority in this manner. At the same time, it would be biblical to make an appeal to him individually concerning the relational difficulty.

This was the proper attitude that Paul encouraged the Colossian believers to have when he wrote Colossians 3:22, *"Servants, obey in all things your masters according to the flesh; not with eyeservice, as menpleasers; but in singleness of heart, fearing God."* God will honor his child who displays this attitude towards his authority and will hear and answer his prayer.

On the other hand, we often find ourselves needing to pray for someone who is a friend, relative, co-worker, new believer, or someone under our authority. In this situation we are the spiritual leader, and it is our responsibility to recognize how God would want us to pray for them. In prayer, and through counsel, we need to know how to meet them where they are in their ditch (get down into it with them) and take them to where they need to be: we need to lead them out of their ditch. This is the truth that the Apostle Paul sought to convey when he wrote to the Galatians, *"Brethren, if a man be overtaken in a fault, ye which are spiritual, restore such a one in the spirit of meekness; considering thyself, lest thou also be tempted."* (Galatians 6:1) We who are spiritually mature need to help the spiritually immature by interceding for them according to Scripture.

The People for whom we are to pray

Authority — The Bible directs us to pray for some people and assumes that we will pray for others. In I Timothy 2:1, the Bible teaches that the four types of prayer should be made for all men (i.e., all mankind in general). This would include our neighbors, our co-workers, church members, and family members, etc. Next, this passage says that we should pray for kings. In our modern day government this would direct our attention to our government officials on local, state, and national levels: we need to be praying for our mayors, police officers, senators, governors, state and national representatives, and our President. In recent months, I sent a copy of my commentary on Galatians to our President, George W. Bush, to add to his personal library for assistance in his Bible study times. I also sent him a personal note to encourage him, that as a faithful Christian citizen, I would continue to pray for him on a regular basis. Just a few weeks later I received a card in the mail from the White House that had the following words, "Thank you for keeping us in your prayers. We are encouraged knowing we have your support. Please keep our great nation in your prayers and may God bless you." It closed with a copy of his and his wife's signature.

Fellow believer, it is our duty to intercede on behalf of our governing authorities that God has set up before us. According to Romans 13, they are His personal representatives in our lives. Here Paul mentions "all that are in authority." This would include your pastor, your parents (if you are a child), public servants, and bosses. Below is a sample prayer based on Scripture that can be prayed for any person who is an authority in your life. If you are a married woman, I would especially like to encourage you to pray this prayer, or one similar to it, for your husband on a regular basis. Remember, when you pray God's will for him, and God answers your prayers you will benefit from it, too. If you know the specific areas of strengths and weaknesses of the person in authority, then I encourage you to write out a scriptural-based prayer that you, from your heart, pray on their behalf daily. The prayer I have written is:

> Father, in the name of the Lord Jesus Christ, we give thanks to You for the leader _____ that You have given to this _____ of ours. We believe that he has been ordained to this position of authority by You and his power is only an extension of You. Although we do not understand all of the ramifications of Your truth, we trust You that he is Your minister for good. (Romans 13:1-4) . We lift him up to You as a needy individual.

First, we ask that You would challenge his heart with the truth of his need of accepting Jesus Christ as his personal Savior. We believe that it is Your will that all men would be saved (1 Tim. 2:4). If he is already saved, Father, please help him to see his need of obeying You today and hearkening to Your still small voice. Your Word tells us that the king's heart is in Your hand. We are trusting You to turn it today in the direction that You will it to go (Prov. 21:1).

Even as we lift him up to You, we ask that You would give him wisdom and discernment to make God-fearing and God-honoring decisions. Help him to display the character of Christ to those around him; especially to his children, the next generation. We ask that You would guide and guard him today and help him to recognize himself to be Your servant (Psalm 127:1, Jer. 27:6). Father, we ask that you would bring his marriage into agreement with Scripture: He is to love his wife whole-heartedly as Christ loved the Church and gave Himself for it. Help him to love his wife and treat her as a delicate vessel without getting angry or bitter at her. Help him to represent You faithfully, Heavenly Father, to his children by bestowing his favor and blessing upon them today. Please caution him so that he will not provoke his children to wrath but will rather bring them up in the nurture and admonition of You, not being used of the enemy to offend them and thus to misrepresent You. Thank You for him and for his ministry. Please bless him as You best see fit today and only as You can. Amen.

A few years ago I preached on this specific truth of intercession to the church I was a member, and I shared this prayer with the people. I heard many positive responses over the next few weeks. One lady, in particular, stands out in my mind.

She stopped me at the back of the auditorium one evening and said, "Harry, do you remember the prayer that you handed out a couple of weeks ago on praying for your authority?" I said, "Yes." She became all excited and got this broad smile on her face; her countenance beamed as she said, "Well, I've been praying it for my husband daily since you preached, and I'm seeing real changes in his life." Tears came to her eyes as she encouraged me to keep preaching strongly on this theme. Our God is a prayer-hearing and answering God. Spurgeon once said, "I would rather be the Master of the Art of Prayer than M.A. of both universities (Oxford and Cambridge). He who knows how to pray has his hand on the leverage which moves the universe."[1] The key to effectively interceding for another is to know how to pray for them and then to pray for them on a regular basis.

Others — God also gives directions in Scripture regarding other people that we are to pray for. This would include laborers for the harvest of lost souls, fellow church members, your enemies, your wife, your children, etc.

Laborers for the Harvest — Too often, in our churches today, believers focus on the lost of this world only around the time of a missions conference or when a missionary is visiting on deputation (or home on furlough) and shows his slides and gives an update. Those meetings raise our interest and excitement about reaching lost souls "out there," and we anticipate what God will do through them on their mission field; but when Jesus Christ got excited about lost souls and was moved with compassion towards them, it was not the "them out there" but the "these here and now." The Bible records the incident in Matthew 9:35-38 which reads,

"And Jesus went about all the cities and villages, teaching in their synagogues, and preaching the gospel of the kingdom, and healing every sickness and every disease among the people. But when he saw the multitudes, he was moved with compassion on them, because they

fainted, and were scattered abroad, as sheep having no shepherd. Then saith he unto his disciples, The harvest truly is plenteous, but the laborers are few; Pray ye therefore the Lord of the harvest, that he will send forth laborers into his harvest."

Notice here that Jesus' heart was moved when he personally viewed the multitudes of people about him who were lost as a sheep without a shepherd. We are now saved; and as Peter states it in 1 Peter 2:25, *"For ye were as sheep going astray; but are now returned unto the Shepherd and Bishop of your souls."* We who are saved have returned to the Shepherd of our souls; yet how many people do we run across daily that are going about as lost sheep without a shepherd. Today I went out to eat lunch with some men from our church. We gave the waitress a gospel tract and told her that within this tract were Biblical directives on how a person could know he was going to heaven. She asked us if she could keep it, turned around , walked about ten steps away, then stopped what she was doing so she could read the tract. She was interested in it and wanted to know what the Bible said. When Jesus saw the people personally, he turned to his disciples and with great passion (for His purpose in life is to seek and to save that which is lost) said to His disciples, *"The harvest truly is plenteous."* There is no lack for souls in this world who need to be saved, and the fields are ripe for harvesting!

On different occasions I've driven through the sate of Kansas from east to west on I-70 and north to south on I-35. I remember one time when our bus had left for an adult missions trip about 5:00 p.m., and we were traveling south on I-35. The sun was setting in the west, and wheat fields were in abundance. As the sunlight radiated off of the wheat fields (which were all you could see from the edge of the road to the horizon), I could not help but be reminded of what Christ said, *"The harvest truly is plenteous, but the laborers are few; Pray ye therefore the Lord of the harvest, that he will send forth laborers into his harvest."*

Seeing lost people come to Christ is very near the heart of our God. When Christ, full of compassion, challenged and compelled the disciples, the pillars and the foundation of the church, to pray for laborers to reap the harvest of souls in the field of humanity, He was speaking to every generation in the church age. It was not their responsibility alone to pray for more laborers for the harvest. It is ours, too.

I preached from this passage while preparing our people for an upcoming missions conference, and I never shall forget the conviction that gripped my soul as I preached. The Holy Spirit spoke to my heart in a very real way and asked, "Harry, do you pray for God to send forth laborers into the harvest on a regular, daily basis?" Inside, in my mind's eye, I hung my head in shame and thought, "How did I miss this most necessary ingredient in winning lost souls to Christ?" Needless to say I took part in the invitation that night, responding to the message from the Lord.

So let me ask you, fellow believer, "Do you pray for God to send forth laborers into His eternal harvest on a regular basis?" I know how it is. We get caught up in the hustle and bustle of day-to-day life, and the important things take a back seat to those that have become urgent. Even though the urgent very rarely have great impact on eternity, we allow our focus to turn toward them anyway, losing sight of God's purpose for us as believers (to be salt and light). God wants us to pray for Him to send forth laborers into the harvest; in fact, He commanded us to do so. We must intercede for laborers so that we can reach our generation for Christ.

Our Enemies — As Christ was giving the Sermon on the Mount, He spoke truths that seemed to go against normal human responses. In Matthew 5:43-44 Jesus said,

"Ye have heard that it hath been said, Thou shalt love thy neighbor, and hate thine enemy. But I say unto you,

Love your enemies, bless them that curse you, do good to them that hurt you, and pray for them which despitefully use you, and persecute you."

As you read these verses you may find yourself having some of the same thoughts that those Jews listening to Christ had. "Pray for my enemies — yeah, I'll pray for them all right. I'll pray that God gets them with hell fire and brimstone." Yet notice with me exactly what Christ is saying. He wants us to bless those who curse us, those people who have offended us; and, if Christ were standing here right now, He would instruct us to pray God's blessing upon them. (And you know who they are because their names or faces have passed through your mind.) One evening after church I was cornered by a lady who wanted to pass on some information to me. After a long day, I assumed this lady had good news. I was wrong. I had been lured into this conversation by a facade of congeniality; but, as we talked, her attitude became more carnal, and she displayed to me a rude attitude that was really meant for someone else. There was that negativity and critical spirit (that we all abhor to have directed our way) and the offering of unsought-for counsel. When I walked out to my vehicle, I was tempted to pick up her foul attitude; but just then the Holy Spirit reminded me to pray a blessing on this lady. On my way home, as I was reminded of the injustice she had done me, I continued to pray a special blessing from God on her life — that God would soon make Himself real to her in a positive way. As I prayed for her, God released me from the natural human tendency to wish to get even in some way. I was refreshed and rejoicing by the time I got home. I do not know if God ever blessed her in answer to my prayer (I'm sure He did), but I do know that I was definitely blessed after I prayed for her. This was also true for someone in Scripture. God not only turned the captivity of Job and stopped the trial that Job was going through, but He blessed him as well. Job 42:10 states, *"And the Lord turned the captivity of Job, when he prayed for his friends: also the Lord gave Job twice as much as he had before."* Let me remind you that these "friends" had just spent conversation after conversation attributing Job's trial to secret sin and accusing him of having sin in his life. As Job's counselors, they misrepresented God; and God held them accountable for their misguided counsel.

God wants us to pray for our enemies, those who offend us. He wants us to bless them and do good to them. I have written the following prayer which may help you to properly handle a torn relationship with someone that you might know (and are thinking of now):

Heavenly Father, _____ has offended me by doing/saying _____. I know that you are aware of all that happens and nothing is a surprise to you. Please grant me the grace and the strength to forgive him for this offense and any like it that might occur in the future. I choose to forgive him completely right now. Lord, please help me to look for ways to meet his needs. Help me to fulfill Scripture and to be a blessing to him. Help me to overcome any and all evil that he has done by doing good to him. In the name of your precious Son, Jesus Christ, and through His blood. Amen.

Church Members — In almost all of Paul's epistles written to churches or fellow believers, he presented that he was praying for them. In Romans 1:8-9 he wrote, "First, I thank my God through Jesus Christ for you all, that your faith is spoken of throughout the whole world. For God is my witness, whom I serve with my spirit in the gospel of his Son, that without ceasing I make mention of you always in my prayers." Here in Romans, as he did in many other places in Scripture, the first thing that he told them was that he was faithful to express his gratefulness to God on their behalf. He wrote a statement very similar to that written to the Corinthians in 1 Corinthians 1:4 which states: *"I thank my God always on your behalf, for the grace of God which is given you by Jesus Christ."* He also mentioned his prayers for them to the believers at Ephesus, Philippi, Colosse and Thessalonica, and in his second letter to Timothy (1:3) he wrote, *"I thank God, whom I serve from my forefathers with pure conscience, that without ceasing I have remembrance of thee in my prayers night and day."* He told Timothy that he prayed for him daily, both at morning time and evening. Praying for fellow church members was very important to Paul. Many of these churches he himself had established, but not all. Yet, when he wrote to them under the direction of the Holy Spirit, he told them he prayed for them.

Paul believed in praying *for* fellow believers; he also believed in the prayers *of* his fellow believers. In Philemon 1:22 Paul wrote to Philemon, *"But withal prepare me also a lodging: for I trust that through your prayers I shall be given unto you."* He had confidence in the prayers of his fellow believers. While writing to the believers at Thessalonica in his first epistle to them he simply stated, *"Brethren, pray for us"* (I Thessalonians 5:25).

Not only was the Apostle Paul a strong advocate of fellow believers praying for one another, but certain laymen were as well. In Colossians 4:12, Paul encourages the Colossian believers by telling them expressly how Epaphras was praying for them. Colossians 4:12 states, *"Epaphras, who is one of you, a servant of Christ, saluteth you, always laboring fervently for you in prayers, that ye may stand perfect and complete in all the will of God."* As Epaphras prayed for them Paul described his prayer life as always laboring fervently for them. What a testimony he was! It must have been quite an example and encouragement to the Colossian believers.

We need to be praying fervently for the needs of our fellow believers. We need to be lifting them up in prayer and supporting them. It would not hurt from time to time to tell them this, either. On one occasion, while working in another ministry, I sent anonymous notes to my supervisor and coworkers, telling them that someone was praying for them. If someone in your church received an anonymous note from you telling them that you were praying for them, do you think it would encourage them? Would you be encouraged if you received a note from someone of this nature? I believe that if we would spend more time praying for one another, we would not hear about as many church conflicts as we do. The energy we expend quarrelling could be much better spent praying.

Wife — In 1 Pet 3:7 the Bible directs husbands, *"Likewise, ye husbands, dwell with them according to knowledge, giving honor unto the wife, as unto the weaker vessel, and as being heirs together of the grace of life; that your prayers be not hindered."* The last phrase speaks volumes on how God will respond to the husband who does not treat his wife with the proper respect. God simply says, "If you mistreat your wife, I will not answer your prayers." If this be the case, as strong as God is, then it behooves us as men to be sensitive to the needs of our wives and to be in tune with them emotionally and spiritually, so that we may lead them gently. A man will not be very sensitive to his wife's needs naturally. That is why, in Ephesians, God commanded husbands to love their wives. When it is commanded by God to the New Testament believer, it can only truly be obeyed from the heart in obedience to the Spirit of God. When a man is insensitive to the needs of his wife, he is focused on himself and his goals and desires, and not on her. He is first in his life and she is not. One Scriptural remedy for this is to pray for your wife daily. If a man is praying for his wife's needs daily, and interceding for her, then he will be more in tune with her needs and will have a greater desire to meet those needs. Following is a prayer that is simply based on Scripture:

> Heavenly Father, thank You for the wonderful, prudent wife that You have given to me. Truly, in her, You have shown me Your favor. Today, Lord, I ask that You would place a hedge of protection about her and protect her from all of the wiles of the enemy. Show me,

Lord, if there are any holes in my umbrella that might hinder her spiritual growth today. Please seal them up. Show me how I can better make my heart to trust her.

Father, I humbly confess that the love that I have toward my wife is limited to myself. Your Word instructs me to love my wife as Christ loved the Church and gave Himself for it. Please show me the areas of my life in which I lack this heavenly, Christ-like love for her. I ask that your Holy Spirit would please keep me accountable for the words that I say to her, the attitudes that I display to her, and the actions that I do for her so as to fulfill this Scripture in my life.

Father, I ask that You would show me if there are any areas of bitterness that I might have toward my wife so that I can confess them and forsake them right now, making our fellowship sweeter in Christ. Lord, Your Word commands that my wife reverence me. Please help me to be the right kind of a husband so as to make this easy for her to do. Help me to honor my wife today by treating her delicately as a precious piece of fine crystal. Father, I ask that You would bless my wife in all of her duties and responsibilities today. In your Son's precious name and through His blood. Amen.

Our Children — The Bible says in Psalm 127:3, *"Lo, children are an heritage* [inheritance] *of the Lord: and the fruit of the womb is His reward."* I must confess that when we are driving down the road, and my wife and I are trying to have an important conversation, this is not the verse that comes to mind when two of our children are pestering one another, fussing, and whining. Yet, what an important truth for all of us who are parents. Children are God's inheritance to us, and we must do our best to represent Him to them. Praying a prayer similar to the following would help us keep the right frame of mind as we work with them and invest in them.

Heavenly Father, thank You for the children with whom You have blessed me and whom You have placed under my care in this life. I esteem them as a stewardship from You for which You will hold me accountable for one day. Thank You for the reward that they are in our home. Help me not to be an unwise steward, but to seek Your guidance and heart toward them as I train them up to fear You.

I realize that my training them properly includes teaching them to love and respect You, disciplining them in love, and living the right example in front of them. This is an awesome responsibility. Please help me not to esteem it lightly.

You command my children to obey their parents in all things, Lord; give them the grace to do this. Guard me, as their father, so I do not provoke them to anger or discourage them, thus harming the way they view You. Please allow Your Holy Spirit to caution them not to rebel so as not to bring a curse upon their lives. Help me, as the parent, to train them up in the nurture and admonition of You so that they will desire to have a relationship with you at an early age. Help my wife and me make our home a haven of rest for our children. Keep them from the evil one, place a hedge of protection about them and enlarge my umbrella (as their authority) so that Satan cannot wound them. Please bless them today, and allow them to see that You are at work in their lives. It's in your Son's name and through His blood that I pray all these things. Amen.

It is the privilege of born again children of God to take time to talk to their Father on behalf of others. Please do not esteem intercessory prayer lightly, or take it for granted and neglect it. God can use you mightily in the lives of those around you if you will let Him.

Commitment Prayer

Heavenly Father, please help me to be sensitive to pray for those who you bring to mind and for their needs. I do not wish to simply think about them or talk about them, but to pray for them. I recognize that praying for those in authority and those under my authority is the most important way that I can influence their lives. Thank You for Your gentle reminder. In Jesus' name, amen.

---

[1] Internet site, www.bible.org.

Prayer and Fasting

So the people of Nineveh believed God, and proclaimed a fast and put on sackcloth, from the greatest of them even to the least of them; And God saw their works, that they turned from their evil way; and God repented of the evil, that he had said that he would do unto them; and he did it not.

— Jonah 3:5,10

AFTER JONAH OBEYED GOD and went to Nineveh, the people of Nineveh became more serious about their relationship with God than anything else. From the king down to the least of the people, the whole city fasted and put on sackcloth as a symbol of repentance before God. God had stated to Nineveh through the prophet Jonah that if Nineveh did not repent, he would destroy their city. In this chapter we will see Biblical examples of fasting and practical tips concerning fasting.

Biblical (Christian) fasting is a form of self-denial, deliberate abstinence from some or all food for a spiritual purpose that demands a deep level of commitment and sacrifice. Another way to describe fasting is putting God first in your life in a very intense way for a specific period of time and for very definite spiritual purposes.

Nehemiah was one man in the Old Testament that saw God work mightily through his authority in response to Nehemiah's fast. Another Jewish brother had been to Jerusalem and came back to Babylon. When he came back he described the ruins of Jerusalem to Nehemiah who was the king's cupbearer. Nehemiah 1:4 says, *"And it came to pass, when I heard these words, that I sat down and wept, and mourned certain days, and fasted, and prayed before the God of Heaven."* In the prayer that is recorded in Scripture, Nehemiah appealed to God on behalf of Israel's sin. He reminded God that He had promised Moses that if Israel would repent of their sins and turn to Him, then God, who had scattered them, would bring them back into the land of their inheritance again. In response to Nehemiah's prayer and fasting, which was a result of his burden for Jerusalem, God worked in the heart of the king of Babylon and allowed Nehemiah the opportunity to go back to Jerusalem and rebuild the walls. He also got to do this with his expenses being paid by the king of Babylon. Nehemiah was intense in his burden and his prayer to the point of fasting, and God heard his prayer and answered it.

In my senior year of Bible college, Bill, a friend of mine who was studying for the ministry, was praying about God's timing on going to the mission field. I remember talking to him about it and agreeing to pray for him. He confided in me that he had committed to pray and fast about it for five days. Over the course of the next two months, things really got exciting for Bill. His schedule picked up. He began candidating for this field and God answered his prayer requests. Before he graduated, he had no money in monthly support. Within one and a half years, he was on the mission field in Mexico with *full support*. God had responded to his prayer and fasting.

Other men in the Bible noted for fasting were Jesus (he fasted for 40 days in the wilderness), Moses (who fasted for 40 days on Mt. Sinai at the receiving of the law), Ezra (who prepared his heart to seek God and confessed the sins of the nation of Israel to God on their behalf), Daniel (who prayed and fasted for 21 days). From the beginning of Daniel's prayer, God heard and sent an angel to answer him. This angel said that he had been hindered by another angel, the prince of Persia. After he prayed and fasted for 21 days, God heard and answered Daniel's prayer request.

In October of 2000, God gave me the opportunity to go to Guyana, South America, and preach at a crusade for one of our missionaries, Dr. Greg Waller. Starting about two weeks before our meetings, different people came to me privately and said, I don't know what God is planning to do on your trip, but I have been led to pray and fast for you before you go and while you are there. One of my closest friends, another minister in Georgia, committed to pray and fast for me every day that I was to preach. I had even fasted and prayed in preparation not knowing what to expect. God was very gracious. I would have been thrilled to see five or six people saved if God so chose, but He had a greater blessing in store. Tuesday was the first night of the crusade and God permitted us to see three or four people pray and ask Jesus Christ to save them for the first time in their lives. On Wednesday night, when we got off the boat (to get to the church we had to travel seven miles up a river and get out and walk 300 yards), there were two people waiting for us at the tent who said they came to learn how they could get saved. This happened an hour before the meetings began. Then the Lord blessed the preaching that night with another two or three people who for the first time ever asked Christ to save them. Wednesday night my heart was very heavy in prayer for the crusade and especially that God would send lost people. In fact, Thursday morning when I awoke until about noon, my heart was still very heavy and I could not eat. At noon, I realized why my heart was so heavy. Located in the village of Moreshee was a little one-room school house. The people of the village are mainly Hindu and Muslim with some Christians. The head school teacher (who was Muslim) agreed to let me and the two gentlemen with me, Mark Anderson and Glenn Booth, come and minister to the children in song and preaching. God harvested seven children's souls that afternoon in a Hindu public school, and He wasn't through yet. When we went to the tent to prepare for the services, there were two more people waiting on us who had not been saved who came there wanting to know about salvation. After I preached that night, eight people (six of whom it was their first night at the crusade) trusted Christ as their Savior. By the end of the crusade, a total of 36 people had trusted Christ, and many Christians had made decisions for Him. I knew the results could only have been God's answers to the prayers of His people. When God's people get serious with Him on His terms, through prayer and fasting, God answers their prayers.

Maybe you have thought about fasting and praying. Probably the most common is a no-food-or-juice fast for one day. This is the type of fast on which a person only drinks water throughout the day and eats nothing nor drinks anything else. When on a no-food fast, it is important that the time that you would normally give to eating your meals you donate to special times of prayer. Thus the habit of prayer and fasting. This discipline of the body and soul are making the statement to God that your nearness to Him in prayer and the request that you are bringing before Him are more important to you than your natural desires for food.

Other types of fasts are fellowship and sleep fasts. Whether it is on a half-day, an overnight, or a couple of days, scheduling time away from family and friends to get alone with God can be very beneficial. I know some pastors and evangelists, friends of mine, that commonly take a couple of days apart a year to get alone with God away from everyone else to receive God's direction for the upcoming year. These times apart have had vital impacts on their ministries. Jesus himself sometimes in the midst of His ministry had fellowship fasts. There were times when even his disciples were sent away so that He could spend time alone with His Heavenly Father. Mark 6:46 states, *"And when He had sent them away, he departed into a mountain to pray."* The "them" here refers to His disciples. Jesus sent away those closest to Him at this point: he fasted from His human fellowship so that He could have heavenly fellowship.

Another type of fast is a no-sleep fast. Sometimes while prayer for upcoming revival services, we have assigned certain hours of the day that each person will designate as their hour of prayer for revival. Sometimes this means that a person will get the 2:00-3:00 or 3:00-4:00 a.m. shift. If they are usually awake at this time, then they are placing a higher priority on prayer for revival, time alone with God, than they are on their body's natural needs for sleep. A person can also dedicate whole nights in prayer to God. Jesus, before choosing the twelve disciples, went apart and prayed all night. Luke 6:12 reads, *"And it came to pass in those days, that he went out into a mountain to pray, and continued all night in prayer to God."*

Each of these types of fasts are biblical. It is important that if God leads you to fast or challenges your faith for you to fast that you do it, but be sensitive to His leading.

Another important facet of fasting that you might wonder about is the length of the fast. The length of the fast must be directed by God. In Isaiah 58:5, God asked the question, *"Is it such a fast that I have chosen?"* This is the most relevant aspect. If God did not lead you to fast then you must put that before the Lord and wait for His direction. Fasting from food can be as short as one meal or as log as forty days with no food. Some variations that are found in the Bible are a one day fast. Esther, Mordecai and some Jews, the Apostle Paul, and the city of Nineveh all fasted for three days. Daniel fasted for three weeks. Jesus, Moses, and Elijah all went for forty days without food. Other Bible characters such as Ezra, Nehemiah, the church at Antioch, and Joshua and the elders of Israel are noted for fasting but the amount of time is not mentioned.

God warns people in Scripture not to abuse fasting. In the early section of Isaiah 58 God warned Israel not to fast to earn

God's blessing. Later on in that same chapter God warns Israel not to fast as a substitute for obedience. In Luke 18:11-12 Jesus tells the story of a Pharisee who stood and prayed, *"God, I thank thee, that I am not as other men are, extortioners, unjust, adulterers, or even as this publican. I fast twice in the week, I give tithes of all that I possess."* As Jesus was describing this incident He was telling people not to be like this pharisee. Two truths that I believe God would have us to glean here about fasting are: 1) Do not fast to impress others, and 2) Do not fast as a form of ritualism. While fasting is a legitimate spiritual exercise, it is not accepted by God if motivated by the wrong purpose.

Maybe as you've been reading the question may have come to mind, "Why should I fast?" Following are some biblical reasons to fast and references to substantiate it: 1) Fast to please the Lord (Zechariah 7:5), 2) Fast in response to God's call (Joel 1:14), 3) Fast to humble yourself before God (Psalms 35:13), 4) Fast to seek God's face more fully (Jeremiah 29:13), 5) Fast as a holy discipline for your soul, and 6) Fast for the freedom of another held in bondage by the enemy (Mark 9:29 "And he said unto them, This kind can come forth by nothing, but by prayer and fasting." Each of the above reasons is both biblical and important. As a child of God you want to make sure that if God leads you to fast you know why you are fasting. Go to His Word and confirm it. My prayer is that God will use this to encourage you to draw closer to Him in this area and that as you do you will be blessed by Him.

Commitment Prayer

Heavenly Father, please help me to be careful to fast when you want me to for the right reasons and not to abuse this privilege. In Jesus' name, amen.

12

Five Reasons God Will Not Answer Our Prayers

"If I regard iniquity in my heart, the Lord will not hear me."
— Psalm 66:18

BECAUSE the most important relationship a believer has is his relationship with God, the Bible gives clear indication that there are reasons fellowship with Him may be hindered and prayers may not be answered. In this chapter we are going to probe into five different reasons that God will not answer a person's prayers. We want to be careful that none of these reasons are found to be true in our lives.

Disobedience

In the first chapter of Deuteronomy, the Israelites were reminded of what happened when they were commanded of God to go into the promised land and defeat the foe. They were to begin by going in and fighting the Amorites. However, when ten of the twelve spies came back with a negative report, the children of Israel were discouraged and decided not to go up and fight. God then directed them toward the wilderness by way of the Red Sea; but at that point they decided to suit up for battle and fight the Amorites (despite God's command). They fought the Amorites and were sorely defeated. The Bible describes the Amorites chasing the Israelites as if they were a bunch of angry bees following their enemy. Israel then returned, prayed and cried out to the Lord. However, God's response was not favorable; in fact, He would not even listen to them. Deuteronomy 1:45 reads, *"And ye returned and wept before the LORD; but the LORD would not hearken to your voice, nor give ear unto you."* They had directly disobeyed the Lord and now He would not even *hearken* to their voices. Not only did they disobey, but they were defeated as well. Many Israelites lost their lives, and then when they turned to God in prayer, He would not listen to them.

Have you disobeyed God recently? Does it seem like God has shut His ear from hearing you? Are you seeing real defeat because of your disobedience? It is time to repent and turn back to God, humbly asking His forgiveness. God will not hearken to our prayers when we disobey Him.

Secret Sin

Psalm 66:18 states, *"If I regard iniquity in my heart, the Lord will not hear me."* Here the Psalmist acknowledges on paper what he has learned about God. The word, "regard," in this verse has the understanding of beholding it but not repenting of it; or to see it and approve of that sin being present in the heart or the inner being of man. Notice where this sin is located, it is in the heart. Sins of the heart seldom stay there; yet the psalmist confirms for us while writing under the inspiration of God that our sins will keep God from hearing our prayers. If we willfully choose not to condemn and confess the sin that is in our hearts then God will not hear us. We believers need to be careful what we allow to fester in our hearts. This secret sin could be wrong thoughts that we choose to dwell on, emotions and attitudes that do not please God, or just plain willful stubbornness. One thing is clear: if we regard iniquity in our hearts, or secret sin, God will not hear or answer our prayers.

Indifference

The book of Proverbs describes varying types of people and circumstances with which a person may find himself associated. In the latter part of Proverbs 1 God describes a situation between Himself and an unwise person. God portrays here an individual who has gotten off target and has sinned. God first tries to reprove the individual; yet he is indifferent towards God and rejects Him. He tries to counsel the person — he refuses. God tries and tries and tries, by way of wisdom and from every angle to warn him against impending punishment yet he remains disinterested. Then when his circumstances heat up and everything falls in on him, he wants to cry out to God for help. However, God plainly states in verse 28, *"Then shall they call upon me, but I will not answer; they shall seek me early, but they shall not find me."* Please, fellow believer, heed the simple reproofs of life and the basic warnings that God gives you through His counselors, godly people, and His Word. Be careful to take His counsel. Do not ignore Him when He speaks truth to your heart. For if you do you may find yourself in dire circumstances you never dreamed you would face. If you are indifferent to God's counsel when you face trouble and decide you need Him then, He will not hear you and He will not answer you.

Neglect of Mercy

Have you ever had the opportunity to help someone yet didn't? I remember one time when, as an older teenager, I was running an errand across town for my parents. As I was going back to my car, this rather seemingly harmless man asked me if he could get a ride back to his neighborhood since his car was in the shop. His home wasn't but a mile or so out of the way and, as I prayed about it on the spot, I had peace that it was okay. The man was only in my car for between five and ten minutes so I took the opportunity to share the gospel with him; had I had a caution in my spirit I would not have given him a ride. Nothing out of the ordinary happened.

God solemnly warns in Proverbs 21:13 that, *"Whoso stoppeth his ears at the cry of the poor, he also shall cry himself, but shall not be heard."* God wants us to be sensitive to those around us, especially those in great need, and to look for ways to help meet such needs. If they ask us to help and we turn a deaf ear to them, God will do so to us when we cry to Him. If we neglect an opportunity to show mercy upon an individual, God will not hear us when we pray. Although no harm was done (and I had the opportunity to once again present the gospel), I would not recommend this as the way to show mercy to others in this day and age.

Self Indulgence

James 4:3 states, *"Ye ask, and receive not, because ye ask amiss that ye may consume it upon your own lust."* Another reason that God says our prayer may not be answered is because we are self-indulgent. It is all too easy to be carnal and pray for something selfishly. We must be careful as believers not to be consumed with our own lustful desires, but to be consumed with what God desires for us. When God is silent to our prayers and self indulgence is present, the problem with our prayers is really ourselves. We are at the center of our prayers and God's will is not. God simply says that we will not receive what we ask for when we pray self-centered prayers. God will not answer prayers based on our own lusts; therefore, be careful, fellow believer, not to pray these types of prayers.

Commitment Prayer

Heavenly Father, I want to know that when I pray, You will hear and answer my prayers. Help me to be sensitive and obedient to Your voice, kind and merciful to those around me, and to pray prayers that are God-honoring and not self-indulging. In Jesus' name, amen.

13

Precepts for Maintaining a Passionate Prayer Life

"Elias was a man subject to like passions as we are, and he prayed earnestly that it might not rain: and it rained not on the earth by the space of three years and six months. And he prayed again, and the heaven gave rain, and the earth brought forth her fruit."

— James 5:17-18

ALL OF US would like to see God answer our prayers in a big way — as He did for Elijah and all of Israel. In order for a believer to have and to maintain a passionate prayer life there are seven precepts to which he must adhere.

Short Accounts

The Christian life is all about relationships. We need to be careful who we communicate with on a regular basis. 1 Corinthians 15:33 says, *"Be not deceived: evil communications corrupt good manners."* Psalm 1:1 reminds, *"Blessed is the man that walketh not in the counsel of the ungodly, nor standeth in the way of sinners, nor sitteth in the seat of the scornful."* God desires us to be careful of our communication and directs us to steer clear of the wrong types of relationships. Relationships are built through communication. And, by the same token, relationships are broken down or strained through lack of communication.

If a believer desires to maintain a passionate prayer life, he must maintain open and free communication with God and those around him. Although we are humans, and humans are sinful people, we cannot go for very long with unconfessed sin in our life. Even though this sin will not affect a believers relationship with God the Heavenly Father, it will hinder and put a strain on his fellowship or prayer time with God.

A believer needs to be ever mindful of keeping short accounts with God. When the Holy Spirit points out a sin in a believer's heart or prompts him about a wrong attitude or action, that is the time the believer should take care of it. 1 John 1:9 is very clear when it states, *"If we confess our sins, he is faithful and just to forgive us our sins, and to cleanse us from all unrighteousness."* God wants us to have free and clear lines of communication with Him. Sin hinders a believer's fellowship with God. 1 John 1:9 was written to believers. When was the last time you confessed sin before God? When was the last time that—as the Holy Spirit prompted you that something was wrong—you took care of it immediately? We need to keep short accounts with God if we are going to maintain a passionate prayer life.

Not only do we need to be concerned about our vertical relationship with God, but our horizontal relationship with man as well. Sometimes, without realizing it, we can offend other people. Just the other day my two boys needed a haircut, and I took them to the barber shop. They got their hair cut and off we went. Our schedule was a little close and we had to go straight to church. The barber and I had been talking and he had even warned me not to speed. I said that I would be careful and would not get in a hurry, but it was just a few minutes away and I was getting a little anxious. I even prayed and asked the Lord to keep me from worrying, trusting Him to get me there on time. Then I went on. I wasn't noticing how fast I was going; I didn't notice when I passed a church member's van in which a young person, who had just gotten his permit, was driving. However, when we arrived at church he was careful to remind me, shouting halfway across the parking lot, that I had passed him doing 45 mph in a 40 mph zone. I didn't notice it; I was focused on the clock. Now he was annoying me. However, Proverbs 6:3 states, *"Do this now, my son, and deliver thyself, when thou art come into the hand of thy friend; go, humble thyself, and make sure thy friend."* So afterwards, I went to him and made right my offense by apologizing.

Matthew 18 tells a believer what to do when he offends another or is himself offended, i.e. go to him and confess it; make it right. When the Holy Spirit speaks, we need to listen being careful to keep short accounts with others. When our relationships with others are strained they will have an impact on our prayer life; they will cool it down. In the sermon on the mount, Jesus taught, (Matthew 5:23-24), *"Therefore if thou bring thy gift to the altar, and there rememberest that thy brother hath ought against thee; Leave there thy gift before the altar, and go thy way; first be reconciled to thy brother, and then come and offer thy gift."* Jesus Christ knew that in order to get our prayers answered we needed to be right with God; and in order to be right with God we must also be right with man. Maintaining a passionate prayer life requires keeping short accounts with God and with man.

Saturate Your Soul with the Word of God

We need to saturate our soul with the Word of God in order to maintain a passionate prayer life. When we are continually in the Word of God for extended periods of time it will have two positive effects on our heart: 1) It will cleanse our hearts, and 2) It will increase our faith.

Ephesians 5:26 states, *"That he might sanctify and cleanse* [purge] *it with the washing* [taking a spiritual bath] *of water by the Word."* This verse lies within a passage that discusses the relationship of Christ and the church. We are His church. Christ wants to cleanse us daily with the washing of the Word in our souls. Sometimes we find that we need this cleansing multiple times throughout the day, yet He is faithful to cleanse us from all unrighteousness every time we go to Him.

Romans 10:17 reads, *"So then faith cometh by hearing, and hearing by the Word of God."* If a born again believer is going to maintain a passionate prayer life he must continue to increase his hearing the Word of God. This isn't simply in the mind. The believer must also have an open heart so that the truth will impact all of his spiritual faculties.

Are you spending time in the Word of God? If not, you ought to be. (This book on prayer can only assist you in your spiritual life, but God's Word will sustain you.) If so, are you spending just short increments of time alone with God in His Word or are you spending longer times in His Word, allowing it to soak into every fiber of your soul? If you want to be cleansed spiritually and have an increase in your faith, then stay in the Word of God; saturating your soul with the Word of God will help you to maintain a passionate prayer life.

Schedule Time Alone with God for Prayer

Another helpful tool to assist us in maintaining a passionate prayer life is our daily planner book. We need to have daily times that we meet with God to talk to Him in prayer. Daniel was a wonderful example of this and had a testimony (even among the heathen with whom he worked) of being a man of prayer. His consistent prayer life landed him in prison with the lions. And the *consistency* of his prayers, as well as his God, was made public when God protected him from the lions all night long. Daniel 6:10 reads, *"Now when Daniel knew that the writing was signed, he went into his house; and his windows being open in his chamber toward Jerusalem, he kneeled upon his knees three times a day, and prayed, and gave thanks before his God, as he did aforetime."* Daniel had built into his schedule times that he met with God in prayer.

I personally wake up early, generally between 4:30 and 5:00 a.m. Our house is quiet then (we have four children). The first thing I do is spend time in prayer with God. I find that with each new day the flesh must surrender anew to the Spirit. If not, I will be tempted to do God's work in my own strength and before I know it, I am offending people as well as being irritable and grouchy. Then my wife is asked the question, "Did you wake up grumpy?" And she responds, "No. I let him sleep in." When I get up, I spend time with God in prayer. Then throughout the day, as the Lord prompts me, I spend time talking with Him. My main time of prayer, however, is in the morning. When I put God first and talk to Him in private, it affects my fellowship with others in public. In order for you to maintain a passionate prayer life you need to schedule time alone with God for prayer.

Spirit-led Prayers

In a previous chapter I explained this to a greater degree. Here I just want to remind you that Romans 8:26 states, *"Likewise the Spirit also helpeth our infirmities: for we know not what we should pray for as we ought: but the Spirit itself maketh intercession for us with groanings which cannot be uttered."* If God's wonderful Holy Spirit is interceding for us then He must have a direction in which He prays for us. We need to be in tune with Him when we pray. We need to be quiet and sensitive to His still, small voice. We need to allow His gentle leadings to direct us in our prayer life. When we pray Spirit-led prayers, we will maintain a passionate prayer life.

Seek Persistently

In Matthew 7:7-8, Jesus said, *"Ask, and it shall be given you; seek, and ye shall find; knock, and it shall be opened unto you: For every one that asketh receiveth; and he that seeketh findeth; and to him that knocketh it shall be opened."* Ask, seek, knock. All three of these terms speak of tenacity. If you are going to maintain a passionate prayer life then you must pray persistently. Christ confirms each one of these words of perseverance. To him that asketh it shall be given. He that seeks shall find. To him that knocks, it shall be opened. None of these phrases give the believer a definite time table as to how soon God will answer his prayers, but it does tell him that his prayers will be answered. We need to seek God persistently if we are going to maintain a passionate prayer life.

David Livingstone, missionary to the continent of Africa, was, among many other things, a man of prayer. He was a very respected man not only for his total surrender to the Lord but his commitment to reach the heart of Africa with the gospel of Jesus Christ. He was so committed to this end that he not only spent his life there furthering the kingdom of God, he gave his life physically when his sickened body lost all strength as he pressed forward for Christ. He was most definitely a man who sought God persistently; in fact, seeking God in prayer was his last physical action on this planet. Below is the account of how his assistants last found him.

April 29th was the last day of the great explorer's travels upon earth, and then he had to be lifted from his hut to the palanquin. At last they reached Chitambo's village in Itala, where he had to lie under the eaves of a house in a drizzling rain till a hut could be prepared for him. Then he was laid on a rude bed in a hut for the night. The next day he lay quietly all day, the attendants knowing that death was not far off. During the early part of the night following, nothing occurred to attract attention, but about four in the morning the boy who lay at his door keeping watch called in alarm for Susi, one of his old servants, fearing that their master was dead. By the light of the candle still burning, they saw him kneeling by his bedside as if in the act of prayer, his head buried in his hands on the pillow. Praying as he went, he had gone on his last journey, and without a single attendant. Alone, yet not alone, for

He who had sustained him through so many trials and dangers had gone with him through the "swelling of Jordan," and brought him safe to the celestial country.[1] Truly, he prayed persistently and God answered.

Selfless Humility

When is the last time you had a child or someone under your authority demand something of you? Generally, this is not the case and a proud person who is demanding will not usually get what he wants. This is also true of God. God desires His people to come to Him with a **humble** spirit as well. In 2 Chron. 7:14 God said to Israel, *"If my people, which are called by my name, shall **humble** themselves, and pray, and seek my face, and turn from their wicked ways; then will I hear from heaven, and will forgive their sin, and will heal their land."* Perhaps the most important response of God here is that He will hear from heaven. When a person prays or cries out to God they want to know that He is listening and that He will hear their petition.

Our God is a prayer-hearing and prayer-answering God. However, the important quality God requires from His people is selfless humility. If a man is **humble** when he goes to God in prayer he will not demand, but will **submissively** ask for his petition to be granted. Then God will hear and answer the prayer from heaven. When this occurs in our lives we will desire to pray more; we will have a renewed passion for prayer. If we are to continue to have a passionate prayer life we must pray with selfless **humility**.

Expect God to Answer Your Prayers

In Acts 12 the Apostle Peter had been placed in prison. He was a leader for the early church and God had been using him mightily. Acts 12:2 says, *"Peter therefore was kept in prison: but prayer was made without ceasing of the church unto God for him."* Herod had taken both James and Peter and placed them in prison. James had been killed. Yet the church continued praying for Peter. The church prayed to God, trusting Him to answer their prayers. The very night before Herod was going to have Peter brought forth and killed, martyred for the faith, God answered the prayers of the church supernaturally. He sent the angel of the Lord to where Peter was in the inner chamber. The angel loosed the chains from off of Peter's hands and took him out through each gate past the four quaterions of soldiers to the outside of the prison. He then sent Peter away. The church prayed, believing God would answer; and He did.

When you pray, do you wonder if God will answer, or are you convinced He will attend to your prayers? If you are going to maintain a passionate prayer life, then you must **expect** God to answer your prayers when you pray.

Commitment Prayer

Heavenly Father, please forgive me for not maintaining a passionate prayer life in the past. It has been hit and miss. Sometimes more hit and other times more miss. You are so good to us all of the time. Please help me to focus on the areas of my prayer life that I need to adjust and manage properly so that I may continue to have close, intimate fellowship with You on a daily basis. In Jesus' name, amen.

---

[1] Worcester, Mrs. J. H. *David Livingston: First to cross Africa with the Gospel* (Chicago, IL: Moody Press, 1987), 104.

Conclusion

It is my prayer that this book has been a blessing to you. My desire is that God would use it to deepen, strengthen and propel your prayer life and faith in Him. Located in the back of the book are some practical tools to help get you started if you have not spent much time in prayer. There is a basic prayer list and a list of Bible verses that will strengthen your faith in God. Although many times we are very familiar with verses on prayer and our faith, we still need gentle reminders from time to time of what God has said in His Word that we can claim as promises.

Appendix A
Sample Prayer List

1. My Family:
   - Spouse _____
       - God's Protection
       - God's Blessing
   - Children: _____   _____
     _____   _____
     _____   _____
       - God's Direction
       - God's Protection
       - God's Blessing

   - My Struggles: _____   _____
     _____   _____
     _____   _____

   - My Needs: _____   _____
     _____   _____
     _____   _____

   - My Praises: _____   _____
     _____   _____
     _____   _____

   - My Distant
     Relatives: _____   _____
     _____   _____
     _____   _____

2. My Church:
    -My Pastor: _____
    -His Wife: _____
    -His Children: _____   _____
                   _____   _____
                   _____   _____

    -Church Leaders: _____   _____
                     _____   _____
                     _____   _____

        -God's Protection
        -God's Blessing

    -Church
     Missionaries: _____   _____
                   _____   _____
                   _____   _____
                   _____   _____
                   _____   _____

        -God's Protection
        -God's Blessing

3. Unsaved Friends and Family of Church Members:

    _____   _____
    _____   _____
    _____   _____
    _____   _____
    _____   _____

4. Church members Health/Physical/Financial needs:

    _____   _____
    _____   _____
    _____   _____
    _____   _____
    _____   _____

5. Pray that God will send forth laborers for the harvest of lost souls.

6. Miscellaneous:
    -Co-laborers: _____   _____
                     _____   _____
                     _____   _____
                     _____   _____
                     _____   _____

    -Salvation of
      Lost: _____   _____
                     _____   _____
                     _____   _____
                     _____   _____

APPENDIX B

Bible Verses that will assist or increase your faith in prayer

Faith:
Luke 17:5 And the apostles said unto the Lord, Increase our faith.

Romans 10:17 So then faith *cometh* by hearing, and hearing by the word of God.

Romans 14:23 And he that doubteth is damned if he eat, because *he eateth* not of faith: for whatsoever *is* not of faith is sin.

1 Thessalonians 5:8 But let us, who are of the day, be sober, putting on the breastplate of faith and love; and for an helmet, the hope of salvation.

Hebrews 11:1 Now faith is the substance of things hoped for, the evidence of things not seen.

Hebrews 11:6 But without faith *it is* impossible to please *him:* for he that cometh to God must believe that he is, and *that* he is a rewarder of them that diligently seek him.

Matthew 8:13 And Jesus said unto the centurion, Go thy way; and as thou hast believed, *so* be it done unto thee. And his servant was healed in the selfsame hour.

Matthew 9:29-30 Then touched he their eyes, saying, According to your faith be it unto you. *30* And their eyes were opened; and Jesus straitly charged them, saying, See *that* no man know *it.*

Matthew 17:20 And Jesus said unto them, Because of your unbelief: for verily I say unto you, If ye have faith as a grain of mustard seed, ye shall say unto this mountain, Remove hence to yonder place; and it shall remove; and nothing shall be impossible unto you.

Mark 9:23 Jesus said unto him, If thou canst believe, all things *are* possible to him that believeth.

James 1:5-6 If any of you lack wisdom, let him ask of God, that giveth to all *men* liberally, and upbraideth not; and it shall be given him. *6* But let him ask in faith, nothing wavering. For he that wavereth is like a wave of the sea driven with the wind and tossed.

Matthew 8:2 And, behold, there came a leper and worshipped him, saying, Lord, if thou wilt, thou canst make me clean.

Matthew 8:10 When Jesus heard *it,* he marvelled, and said to them that followed, Verily I say unto you, I have not found so great faith, no, not in Israel.

Matthew 21:22 And all things, whatsoever ye shall ask in prayer, believing, ye shall receive.

John 11:3-6 Therefore his sisters sent unto him, saying, Lord, behold, he whom thou lovest is sick. *4* When Jesus heard *that,* he said, This sickness is not unto death, but for the glory of God, that the Son of God might be glorified thereby. *5* Now Jesus loved Martha, and her sister, and Lazarus. *6* When he had heard therefore that he was sick, he abode two days still in the same place where he was.

John 14:12 Verily, verily, I say unto you, He that believeth on me, the works that I do shall he do also; and greater *works* than these shall he do; because I go unto my Father.

Psalms 37:3-5 Trust in the LORD, and do good; *so* shalt thou dwell in the land, and verily thou shalt be fed. *4* Delight thyself also in the LORD; and he shall give thee the desires of thine heart. *5* Commit thy way unto the LORD; trust also in him; and he shall bring *it* to pass.

Proverbs 3:5-6 Trust in the LORD with all thine heart; and lean not unto thine own understanding. *6* In all thy ways acknowledge him, and he shall direct thy paths.

Isaiah 26:3 Thou wilt keep *him* in perfect peace, *whose* mind *is* stayed *on thee:* because he trusteth in thee.

Unbelief:
Matthew 6:30 Wherefore, if God so clothe the grass of the field, which to day is, and to morrow is cast into the oven, *shall he* not much more *clothe* you, O ye of little faith?

Matthew 14:31 And immediately Jesus stretched forth *his* hand, and caught him, and said unto him, O thou of little faith, wherefore didst thou doubt?

Matthew 17:17 Then Jesus answered and said, O faithless and perverse generation, how long shall I be with you? how long shall I suffer you? bring him hither to me.

Mark 4:40 And he said unto them, Why are ye so fearful? how is it that ye have no faith?

Luke 24:25 Then he said unto them, O fools, and slow of heart to believe all that the prophets have spoken:

Prayer:

1 Chronicles 16:11 Seek the LORD and his strength, seek his face continually.

Isaiah 56:7 Even them will I bring to my holy mountain, and make them joyful in my house of prayer: their burnt offerings and their sacrifices *shall be* accepted upon mine altar; for mine house shall be called an house of prayer for all people.

Matthew 7:7-8 Ask, and it shall be given you; seek, and ye shall find; knock, and it shall be opened unto you: 8 For every one that asketh receiveth; and he that seeketh findeth; and to him that knocketh it shall be opened.

Matthew 26:41 Watch and pray, that ye enter not into temptation: the spirit indeed *is* willing, but the flesh *is* weak.

Luke 18:1 And he spake a parable unto them *to this end,* that men ought always to pray, and not to faint;

Romans 8:26-27 Likewise the Spirit also helpeth our infirmities: for we know not what we should pray for as we ought: but the Spirit itself maketh intercession for us with groanings which cannot be uttered. 27 And he that searcheth the hearts knoweth what *is* the mind of the Spirit, because he maketh intercession for the saints according to *the will of* God.

BIBLIOGRAPHY

Burr, Richard A. *Developing you Secret Closet of Prayer*. Camp Hill, PA: Christian Publications, 1998.

Carter, Tom. *2200 Quotations from the Writings of C. H. Spurgeon*. Grand Rapids, MI: Baker Books, 1988.

Chapman, J. B. *Bud Robinson, A Brother Beloved*. St. John, IN: Beacon Hill Press, 1989.

Elliff, Tom. *A Passion for Prayer*. Wheaton, IL: Crossway Books, 1998.

Goforth, Rosalind. *Jonathan Goforth*. Minneapolis, MN: Bethany House, 1986.

Internet site: www.bible.org.

Johnson, William J. *Robert E. Lee, The Christian*. Milford, MI: Mott Media, 1976.
Miller, Basil. *Charles Finney*. Minneapolis, MN: Bethany House, 1991.

Paxton, Sam. *Short Quotations of D. L. Moody*. Chicago, IL: Moody Press, 1961.

Rice, John R. *Prayer: Asking and Receiving*. Murfreesboro, TN: Sword of the Lord, 1970.

Spurgeon, Charles H. *Men and Women of the Old Testament*. Chattanooga, TN: AMG Publisher, 1995.

Swift, Catherine. *Eric Liddell*. Minneapolis, MN: Bethany House, 1990.

Tan, Paul Lee. *Encyclopedia of 15,000 Illustrations*. Dallas, TX: Bible Communications, 1998.

Torrey, R. A. *How to Pray*. USA: Whitaker House, 1983.

Unseth, Benjamin. *John Paton*. Minneapolis, MN: Bethany House, 1996.

Verploegh, Harry. *Prayer: A Holy Occupation*. Nashville, TN: Oswald Chambers Publications, 1992.

Worcester, Mrs. J. H. *David Livingston: First to cross Africa with the Gospel*. Chicago, IL: Moody Press, 1987.

ABOUT THE AUTHOR

Dr. Stanley has enjoyed various ministry opportunities. He assisted in and taught various college level Bible courses at Pensacola Christian College while finishing a Ph.D. in Biblical Studies. The Lord then directed him to Eagle Heights Baptist Church where he was an Assistant Pastor for five and a half years. Presently he is the Senior Pastor of Faith Baptist Church in Selmer, Tennessee.

Dr. Stanley has also written and published a Commentary on Galatians. If you have received a blessing from this book or would be interested in the Commentary on Galatians, you can contact Dr. Stanley at hes2@juno.com.